The Basketball Coaches' Complete Guide to the Multiple Match-Up Zone Defense

John Kimble

ISBN: 1-58518-967-7
Library of Congress Control Number: 2006923649
Cover design: Studio J Art & Design
Book layout: Studio J Art & Design
Front cover photo: Jonathan Daniel/Getty Images

Coaches Choice
P.O. Box 1828
Monterey, CA 93942
www.coacheschoice.com

Dedication

This book is dedicated to all of those who have influenced my personal life. I was brought up by inspirational parents who always taught me to go the extra step, to never be satisfied until the job was done right. I hope I have succeeded in accomplishing that goal with the writing of this book.

This book is also dedicated to all of those who have influenced my basketball coaching life and to all the committed basketball coaches that have spent countless hours at coaching clinics, reading books, and "X-and-O-ing" it with their colleagues. I have been a player, a fan, a teacher, a student, a coach, and a lover of the game.

Finally, this book is dedicated to all of those students of the game who have the same love and passion for the game as I have always had.

Acknowledgments

As a student and a coach of the game, several influences have impacted my coaching beliefs. These influences range from summer basketball camps, coaching clinics, coaching textbooks and written publications, video tapes, observing other coaches' practices, and the countless informal coaching clinics with many other coaches trying to learn just one more drill, defense, or play.

Personal influences in my coaching life have included many of the most top-notch coaches of the game:

- The Iowa Basketball Camp (Lute Olson and Scott Thompson)
- The Doug Collins Basketball Camp (Doug Collins and Bob Sullivan)
- The University of Illinois Basketball Camp (Dick Nagy and Lou Henson)
- The Indiana Basketball Camp (Bob Knight)
- The Kansas State University Basketball Camp (Jim Wooldridge, Mike Miller, Jimmy Elgas, Charles Baker, and Chad Altadonna)
- The Washington State University Cougar Cage Camp (George Raveling, Tom Pugliese, Mark Edwards and Jim Livengood)
- The Illinois State University Basketball Camp (Tom Richardson)
- The Maryville (TN) College Basketball Camp (Randy Lambert)
- The Troy University Basketball Camp (Don Maestri)
- The Oregon State University Basketball Camp (Ralph Miller and Lanny Van Eman)
- The Notre Dame University Basketball Camp (Digger Phelps and Danny Nee)
- The Snow Valley Basketball School (Herb Livesey)
- The Purdue University Basketball Camp (Lee Rose)
- The Dick Baumgartner Shooting Camp (Dick Baumgartner)
- Eastern Illinois University (Don Eddy)
- The Millikin University Basketball Camp (Joe Ramsey)

A few of the most memorable and outstanding speakers I have heard at some of the many coaching clinics I have attended have included: Lute Olson, Doug Collins, Hubie Brown, Bob Knight, Dick Nagy, Don Meyers, and Rick Majerus.

Among the most outstanding authors of coaching books in my experience have been Del Harris, Dean Smith, Bob Knight, and Fran Webster. Lute Olson, Hubie Brown. Don Meyer and Jerry Krause, Del Harris, and Dick Baumgartner have been responsible for some of the most outstanding videotapes I have observed and from which I have learned a great deal. Coaching colleagues with whom I have worked have included Doug Collins, Brian James, Gerry Thornton, Benny Gabbard, Steve Gould, Bob Sullivan, Norm Frazier, Tom Wierzba, Steve Laur, Ron Roher, Will Rey, Mike Davis, Dennis Kagel, Don Eiker, Bob Trimble, Dave Toler, and Ed Butkovich.

I was fortunate to always be involved with tremendous coaching staffs which boasted outstanding coaches, who were as outstanding to me as people and friends (if not more so) than they were as coaches. These good friends include outstanding people such as Benny Gabbard, Mitch Buckelew, Scott Huerkamp, Phil Barbara, Chris Martello, Don Tanney, Les Wilson, Al Cornish, Ron Lowery, John Lenz, Doug Zehr, and Ken Maye. To all of these people, I say, "Thank you for your loyalty, commitment, hard work, and effort!"

I would like to thank the many players I have coached, the extraordinary non-player students who were big parts of the basketball programs—the managers, the student statisticians, the film-takers, the student athletic trainers, and student helpers. I hope that I conveyed to each and every one of them the fact that they were important parts of the program and that they all deserved credit for the successes of their respective basketball programs.

I also want to thank the adults that I have met and become friends with in the different communities where I have coached. These people (contributors, supporters of the program, faithful fans, and loyal friends) participated in the development and the successes of the basketball programs where I coached. Some were parents of players, some were parents of students, and some were just fans of the game. These people are Bob and Ro Flannagan, Ed and Roseanne Moore, Ron and Mary Roher, Dick and Sharon Payne, Don and Bev Hiter, Dave Gregory, Norm Frazier, John and Pam Russell, Ken and Judy Sunderland, Fred Prager, Mark Henry, Carlan and Dee Dee Martin, George Stakely, Charles Owens, Dutch VanBuskirk, Kelly Stanford, and so many other good people.

My supportive wife, Pat, was my biggest source of encouragement, positive reinforcement, and support during the writing of this book. My daughter Emily and my son Adam also were sources of personal encouragement that helped me continue this endeavor. My two brothers, Joe and Jim, also offered support as I slowly progressed through the ordeal of organizing and writing. My parents were always positive role models and constant sources of encouragement and support. Jerry Krause (friend, coach at Gonzaga University, author, and an invaluable source of information) also was of great help and encouragement, as was Murray Pool (former high school coach, current publisher of *Basketball Sense*, friend, and source of information).

Gerry Thornton, longtime friend and fellow student of the game, has affected my coaching career probably more than any other person. Benny Gabbard was the one person who got me started in my junior college coaching career and showed great faith and confidence in me during my first years of coaching junior college basketball. I also wish to thank Mike Willard, who converted all of my many hand drawn diagrams into computer-generated works of professional art.

Contents

Foreword

Having studied, taught, and coached the match-up zone defense, we feel this book can be an outstanding resource for coaching staffs from the junior high school level to the collegiate level.

This book can be an excellent teaching tool to accompany the *Match-Up Defense* video by Lute Olson (distributed by Championship Productions). It should be studied by all three groups of defensive coaches—man-to-man defensive coaches, zone defense coaches, and zone-trap coaches—because the multiple match-up defensive system incorporates portions of all three of these defensive schemes.

Even if coaches study this in-depth book on defense and choose to not implement the match-up into their defensive system, they could still use it to improve their own offensive system. The book is extremely organized and visually contains enough diagrams to clearly present and teach the system to a coaching staff.

The book is written so that the basketball staff need not have any prior knowledge or experience with this type of defense, but could still become outstanding match-up zone coaches. The varied defensive stunts can expand the defensive characteristics of the system as much or as little as the staff chooses.

The book breaks down each aspect of the defense, so every phase of the defense is thoroughly explained. The basic terminology, personnel placement, basic slides, and the overall and individual players' responsibilities are presented in a precise and comprehensive manner for all readers to understand. Several defensive breakdown drills are also illustrated and explained, as well as when, where, and why each drill should be used.

The multiple match-up zone defense system is a simple defensive system that can be expanded quite explicitly and remain uncomplicated enough to grasp, all the while maintaining the appearance to the opposition's offense of an extremely complex defensive system. The most frequent and successful offensive situations that have been faced in games are discussed with viable and successful defensive methods that have been thoroughly explained, which prepares the inexperienced coaching staff a great deal.

This coaching book is a must for every serious basketball coach who is looking to improve himself and his program.

Lute Olson
Head Basketball Coach
University of Arizona

Jim Rosborough
Associate Head Basketball Coach
University of Arizona

Preface

The multiple match-up zone defense was developed with the help of many different successful basketball coaches, who work with different age groups and levels of talent—ranging from junior varsity high school teams to the collegiate Division I men's basketball level. All of these coaches have helped me develop a foundation from which my own ideas, philosophies, concepts, techniques, drills, stunts, and so forth were developed for incorporation into the multiple match-up zone defense package.

Several years ago, Arizona coach Lute Olson developed an outstanding coaching videotape that introduced me to the idea of this match-up zone defense. That tape was instrumental in my initial education and the motivation to learn more about the defense. Without the initial education from this outstanding tape, I probably would have never started studying the match-up and this package of the multiple match-up zone defense would have never happened.

Former UNLV coach Jerry Tarkanian also had a coaching video that helped supplement my early knowledge. Former Slippery Rock coach Bob Bartlett was the first person that I actually ever heard speak about the match-up zone at a coaching clinic. We became match-up zone defense colleagues, sharing thoughts and ideas about the match-up zone defense over the telephone for years. Bartlett introduced me to an outstanding book by former Pitt University coach Fran Webster, entitled *Basketball's Amoeba Defense: A Complete Multiple System*. Former Crestview High School assistant coaches Mitch Buckelew, Phil Barbara, Chris Martello, and Scott Huerkamp were involved in many hours of "X-and-O-ing" during the season, as well as preseason and post-season coaching sessions. Experimenting, observing, evaluating, and analyzing—both in practices and games at Crestview High School—helped contribute to the final product.

These thoughts were put in writing and the first multiple match-up zone defense playbook was sent to coach Lute Olson and former Wichita State University coach Scott Thompson for their review, which both generously did for me. So many different coaches, as well as several Crestview High School players, have helped contribute to the building of the multiple match-up zone defense. I wish to thank each and every person who has helped us develop the match-up not just as a great defense, but also as an outstanding defensive system in itself.

The multiple match-up zone defense can be as basic and simple as any defense, or it can be a sophisticated and multiple defensive scheme that can include a variety of defensive stunts. These stunts can be utilized to either protect the overall defense or to probe the opposition for any hidden offensive weaknesses. Using defensive stunts can change an entire offensive team's mindset and general attitude towards defense.

Most teams take the attitude that the defenses must be reactionary to the opponents' offense, in other words, that they must wait and react to defend the opposition's attack. Many offenses dictate and force defenses to react to its actions.

Utilizing defensive stunts can drastically eliminate that attitude and show a defensive team that they can dictate not only the tempo of the game, but what the offense must do. Using defensive stunts will allow the defense to reverse the normal offensive/defensive relationship, which is that most defensive teams must react to the offensive team as the active agents. The match-up system allows the defense to become the attackers and actors and force the offense to become the reactors. This approach can give the defensive team a great amount of confidence and momentum, and it can become a huge morale boost that can spread to every other defense that is utilized. The stunts can keep an offensive team off balance and prevent any rhythm development necessary for an offensive team to have success. These defensive stunts can help boost the defense, while putting the opposition's offense on its heels. In addition, when stunts are used and specific types of offensive weaknesses are discovered, those weaknesses can easily be attacked often and in a variety of different ways. Thus, the match-up makes the defense more unpredictable and more difficult for an offensive team to solve.

1

Advantages of the Multiple Match-Up Zone Defense

The multiple match-up zone defense is used to help protect, conceal, and minimize the defensive team's weaknesses.

The multiple match-up zone defense is a multiple-defensive scheme that can have a variety of looks, as well as many different types of defensive stunts that can help the defense in the following manners:

- To help cover, hide, and reduce a defensive team's weaknesses
- To accentuate a defensive team's strengths

In addition, the multiple match-up can be used to probe the opposition for its various possible weaknesses and then ultimately attack those weaknesses. These goals can be accomplished by using many different stunts that can be easily used in a sporadic and spontaneous manner during the course of a game.

Before a head coach can implement this defense, he must sell it to his staff and let them know that this defense will require a tremendous amount of time and effort—not only by the players, but by every coach as well. The coaching staff must do the following:

- make a commitment to this defense by thoroughly learning it inside and out
- set an example of their trust and belief in this defense to each and every player in the program

- make sure that the players make the same type of commitment
- teach defensive fundamentals, as well as the various intricacies of the multiple match-up, and sell the multiple match-up to the players
- convince every player that the team will have an edge by using this defense for the reasons previously mentioned and also instruct the team that opposing teams oftentimes are not accustomed to playing against match-up defenses and their opponents' offensive performance will suffer on many occasions as a result

A maximum of five different defensive alignments (which could be viewed by opposing offensive teams as five different defenses) can be used. Cosmetically, these five defenses are different, but to the educated and trained defensive coaching staff and team, all of these defenses have almost the same base defense, with almost identical concepts, techniques, slide coverages, terminology, and responsibilities. Naturally, some small differences are apparent, but basically the major difference is just in appearance. As a result, this defensive package looks multiple, varied, and sophisticated, and appears to be a difficult defense for opposing offenses to break down. In fact, it is somewhat simple to grasp for defensive players. A simple way of naming and identifying the five different match-up defenses can also be achieved by using the following defensive numbering system:

- 0 (or fist)—half-court alignment in a 1-1-3 defensive set (see Diagram 2.1). The 0 zone is the first defense that should be taught and is therefore called the base defense. Once it is successfully taught, stunts for the 0 zone should be added. After the stunts are added, the 2 zone and the 3 zone can also be implemented.
- 2—half-court alignment in a 2-3 defensive set (see Diagram 2.2).
- 3—half-court alignment in a 1-3-1 defensive set (see Diagram 2.3).

The match-up zone defense can also be successfully integrated with full-court pressure, especially using various zone presses such as 1-2-1-1, 2-1-2, or 2-2-1. The full-court defensive package is numbered in the following manner:
- 1 press—full-court pressure defense in a 1-2-1-1 defensive set
- 2 press—full-court pressure defense in a 2-2-1 defensive set
- 3 press—full-court pressure defense in a 2-1-2 defensive set
- 5 press—full-court man-to-man defensive set.

If a full-court press defense was used that then dropped back into a half-court defense, it would have a two-digit defensive name, with the first digit representing the full-court defense and the second number signifying the half-court defense. For example, if a team wanted to run a full-court 1-2-1-1 zone press ("1") and then fall back into the 1-1-3 half-court match-up zone defense ("0"), the defensive call would be "10." If the team wanted to run a full-court 2-2-1 zone press ("2") and then fall back into the half-court 1-3-1 match-up zone ("3"), that call would simply be "23." If only a half-court defense is wanted (without any type of full-court pressure), then the defense would be named with only a single digit. In summary, full-court pressure can definitely (and easily) be run in partnership with the multiple match-up defense package, when a team is physically and mentally able to apply full-court pressure defensively.

If the defensive team lacks athletic ability and cannot match the athletic skill level of the opponents, then the multiple match-up could be a viable answer for the coaching staff. If the defensive team is overmatched by opponents with greater height and/or quickness, again the multiple match-up can offer the defensive team a way of neutralizing the height or the quickness difference. For example, if the defending team lacks the necessary height to match up effectively with the opponents, the multiple match-up can provide a very effective safeguard to help neutralize an opponent's big man and/or offensive inside game by complete fronting of the low post and the constant built-in helpside that supports the fronting post defense. Rebounding problems due to a lack of height can possibly be minimized with an organized set of rules for each defender's box-out responsibilities, which provides excellent angles for each defender to box out the opposition. The multiple match-up also allows defensive teams to be able to put pressure on the basketball with a built-in support system of backup reinforcements, in case the opposing offense defeats the initial ball defender.

The multiple match-up zone defense is used to also accentuate the defensive team's strengths.

If you have a minimal number of defenders that excel in some specific facet of team defense, the multiple match-up is a system that can allow those defenders to constantly perform their specialties and accentuate their strengths while also protecting other defenders that may not be as proficient in the same defensive skills. If the defensive team overall has a strong propensity for mentally handling a multiple defensive system, then the multiple match-up is an excellent defensive system to incorporate (with or without defensive deficiencies).

The multiple match-up zone defense is used to also probe the opposition for various weaknesses and then ultimately attack those weaknesses by using many different stunts.

Many teams have a significant mental block when having to play against match-up zone defenses. The mental hang-up can then be compounded with the various defensive stunts that the match-up zone has in its repertoire As a result, an opponent's offense can be strongly confused and effectively grounded. The entire stunting scheme attacks the mentality of the overall offensive team, while certain stunts attack specific individual weaknesses of particular players.

This book will discuss a total of 17 different stunts. Experience has shown that randomly running a specific stunt or two during an early portion of the game is an excellent way to probe the opposition's offense for previously undiscovered weaknesses. Any newly uncovered weaknesses can then be attacked for the remainder of the game, in various strategic manners.

The 0 zone can be signaled from the bench and passed on to every defender simply by using the raised fist. This signal is symbolic for the base defense of the match-up zone defense in two distinct ways and the symbolism should be used as examples to the players that are learning, practicing, and implementing this defensive system.

First, the fist itself can be thought of as an aggressive and attacking posture, which is very appropriate for this defensive system. Most defenses are a method for the defensive team to counter the opposition's offense only after the opposition normally attacks them. They have to first wait for the offensive team to act in some particular way and must then react in a specific way to stop the offensive team. No rule in basketball says that the defensive team must remain in that passive role of waiting, reacting, and attempting to neutralize and counter those offensive actions. The symbol of the fist can serve not only as the name of the defense, but also as a gesture to convince the defense that they do not have to be the reactors, but can be the actors. The defense can be the team that initiates the action, with the action being as aggressive as they want it to be.

Turning the tables in this fashion causes the offense to become the passive team that must wait and read the defense, and then attempt to come up with an offensive plan to fend off the defensive team's attack. The defensive attack can be as aggressive and as multiple as the defensive team chooses it to be. This new attitude of the defensive team can lead to a great deal of self-confidence and faith in itself, which can in turn lead to a great deal more success.

The second symbol of the fist can be also passed on to the defensive team. When a person looks at a fist, five fingers are kept closely together to form an object of strength, toughness, power, and aggressiveness. Each finger can be symbolic of one of the five individual defenders of the 0 zone. If just one finger (or defender) does not perform his responsibilities, the fist (or 0 zone) loses the majority of its force and strength. Every finger (or defender) must be part of the fist (or the 0 zone) for it to be effective. These two symbolic meanings of the fist may aid a coaching staff in selling the defensive mindset and attitude, as well as the overall multiple match-up zone defensive system, to their players.

The Specific Defensive Alignments and General Placement of Defensive Personnel in the Multiple Match-Up Zone Defense

The multiple match-up zone defense can be executed from the following defensive sets:

- 1-1-3 defensive alignment, called the 0 zone (see Diagram 2.1)
- 2-3 defensive alignment, called the 2 zone (see Diagram 2.2)
- 1-3-1 defensive alignment, called the 3 zone (see Diagram 2.3)

Diagram 2.1

The only difference between the alignments of the 0 zone and the 2 zone is that the first two defenders are in a vertical tandem in the 0 zone while horizontally together in the 2 zone. The only difference between the alignments of the 0 zone and the 3 zone is that the two outside defenders in the back line of the 0 zone have aligned themselves with the back guard of the second line of the 0 zone.

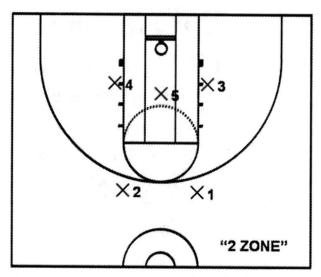

Diagram 2.2

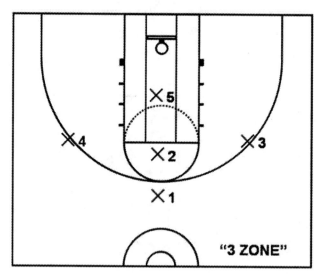

Diagram 2.3

Diagram 2.4 illustrates the minor differences between the 0 zone and the 2 zone. Moving X1 and X2 from a vertical tandem to a horizontal tandem is the only difference. Diagram 2.5 shows the slight changes in the alignments of the 0 zone and the 3 zone, with X3 and X5 walking up to the free throw line extended and being on the second level of the defense (with BG2).

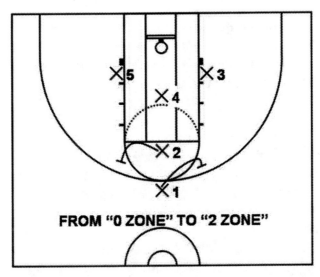

FROM "0 ZONE" TO "2 ZONE"

Diagram 2.4

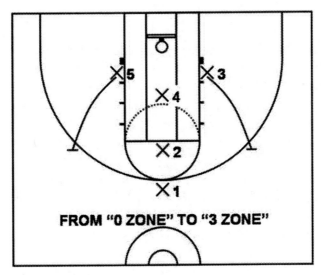

FROM "0 ZONE" TO "3 ZONE"

Diagram 2.5

Regardless of what defensive alignment is used, the match-up zone defense concepts are basically the same. The acronym *TIPS* is used as a "tip" for defensive success. When all five defensive players have the proper *Technique*, *Intensity*, *Positioning* (or location), and *Stance*, then that team will achieve defensive success.

Placement of Personnel

The ball man is any defender that is guarding the player with the ball. The defender should overplay the ball and funnel the ball towards the middle. The overplay on the ballhandler helps reduce the triple-threat capabilities of the ballhandler. Every defensive player should know the proper techniques of pressuring the ball, because at some point during the game, every defender in the zone must be the ball man.

The up guard is the only man in the first line of the 0 zone and the 3 zone (and probably the defender on the defense's left side of the two-man defensive front of the 2 zone). It is believed that the man best suited to play the up guard is usually the team's offensive point guard, or the 1 man (see Diagrams 2.1 through 2.3).

The back guard is the only man in the second line of the 0 zone, the middle man of the second line in the 3 zone, and probably the defender on the defense's right side of the two-man defensive front of the 2 zone. Coaches should utilize their offensive big guard (or 2 man) to become the back guard (see Diagrams 2.1 through 2.3).

The left man is the player to the left (through the eyes of the defense) in the back line of the 0 zone (see Diagram 2.1), and also of the 2 zone (see Diagram 2.2). The left man is the wing player on the defense's left wing in the 3 zone (see Diagram 2.3). The player best suited to the left man position is usually the team's offensive small forward (the 3 man). Since the majority of offenses are right-handed, most initial wing passes are made to the left side of the defense. Therefore, it is preferable to have the majority of the offense's initial wing passes defended by the more mobile of the left man and the right man, which should be the 3 man (versus the 4 man).

The middle man is the player in the middle of the back line in the 0 zone and the 2 zone (see Diagrams 2.1 and 2.2). He should be the lone defender in the third and final line of the 3 zone (see Diagram 2.3). The player best suited to the middle man position is usually the team's offensive center (the 5 man).

The right man is the player on the defense's right side in the back line of the 0 zone and the 2 zone. The right man is the wing on the defense's right side of the 3 zone (see Diagram 2.3). The player best suited to the right man position is usually the team's offensive power forward (the 4 man).

Since the majority of offenses are right-handed, most initial wing passes are made to the defense's left side. Therefore, the majority of the offense's initial wing passes should be defended by the more mobile of the left man and the right man, which should be the 3 man (versus the 4 man). Since the ball is entered on the defense's left side more often than the right side, most shots would then be taken on the defense's left side. Therefore, the back forward on the left side is the key rebounder. The 4 man is most likely a more suitable player than the 3 man in terms of his ability to box out and then to ultimately rebound defensively.

The numbering system that this book will use throughout the remaining chapters will aid your understanding of the defenses. The following designations will be used interchangeably:

- UG1 and X1
- BG2 and X2
- L3, B3, and X3
- M4, F4, and X4
- R5, BF5, and X5

UG1 means the up guard 1 in the match-up. X1 means the point guard on any defense.

BG2 is the back guard in all three zones. X2 is the off-the-ball guard in all three zones.

L3 means the left wing in the 3 zone. B3 means the left forward in the 0 zone (when that defender is on the ball) and the 2 zone. X3 is the small forward in all three zones.

M4 means the middle man in all three zones. F4 means the front man when playing the low post in all three zones. X4 means the 4 man in any of the zones.

R5 means the right wing in the 3 zone defense. BF5 means the back forward in the 0 zone or the 2 zone when the ball is on the opposite side of the court. X5 means the X5 in any of the defenses—especially in some of the stunts.

By using this multiple numbering system, you can see the flow from one zone to another and from one stunt to another—even when the numbering changes in the same explanation. It will help you to visualize the basic zone defense flowing into one of the other zones or a stunt.

In other words, you should look at the number to see the standard defender's numbering. For example, 5 means X5 in standard basketball nomenclature. But if you look at the letter in front of the number, it will reveal the positioning of that defender as well as the zone being run. Thus, R5 tells you that X5 is in the wing position of the 3 zone (1-3-1). If it had been BF5, it would still be X5 and he would be in the back forward position of the 0 zone (1-1-3), or the 2 zone (2-3).

3

Terminology of the Multiple Match-Up Zone Defense

In order for the coaching staff and all of their players to be able to effectively communicate clearly, in a very short and concise manner, a multiple match-up zone terminology has been created. This terminology should be continuously used in practices and game preparation—and especially during games. A philosophy has been developed that all terminology (whether it is offense, defense, or any other basketball terminology) should be very descriptive and short, so that it may be easily spoken, easily heard, and most definitely easily understood.

The *base defense* is simply the standard execution of the defense with the regular defensive slides utilized by all defensive players. No special stunts are part of the base defense.

The *defensive slides* are the movements of defensive players in reaction to the opposition's offensive actions—whether it is passing the basketball, initial alignments of players, or cutting action of players. Specific slides are required to counter particular action(s) by the offense. If defensive players align in the proper position/location in the proper defensive stances and use the correct techniques, the defensive slides will be successful in defending the offense—regardless of what the action actually is.

The *ball man* is any defender that is guarding the player with the ball. He should be able to overplay the ball and pressure the ball to a high degree, because he knows

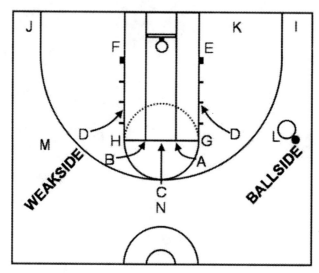

Diagram 3.1

that he has four defensive teammates that will be there to support him if the dribbler breaks him down. The ball man should trace the ball with both hands to put maximum pressure on the ball. Putting constant pressure on the ballhandler helps reduce the triple-threat capabilities of the ballhandler.

With the ball man exerting maximum pressure on the ballhandler, the offensive threat of shooting and passing the ball are both minimized. The remaining threat of driving to the basket should be minimized by the four off-the-ball zone defenders who are in the proper stances and locations to be able to help out. Every defensive player should know the proper techniques of pressuring the ball, because at some point in time, dependent upon the offensive scenario, each defender in the zone will be a ball man.

The *ballside line* is the imaginary line extending from the baseline in the free-throw lane all the way to the actual free-throw line. It is the line that is three feet from the imaginary center line, exactly down the center of the free-throw lane, and is closest to the ballside of the court (see Line A in Diagram 3.1).

The *manside line* is the imaginary line extending from the baseline in the free-throw lane all the way to the actual free-throw line. It is the line that is three feet from the imaginary center line and is exactly down the center of the free-throw lane. It is the line that is furthest from the ballside of the court (see Line B in Diagram 3.1)

The *center line* is the imaginary line that extends exactly down the center of the free-throw lane from the baseline to the free-throw line (see Line C in Diagram 3.1).

The *free-throw-lane line* is the actual line that borders the length of the free-throw lane. It is perpendicular to the baseline and to the actual shooting line in the free-throw lane (see Line D in Diagram 3.1).

The *ballside-block area* is the low-post area near the block on the same side of the court where the basketball is located (see Area E in Diagram 3.1).

The *empty call* is the defensive call made by the back forward telling the front man that no offensive post player is currently in the ballside block area. This call should force the front man to alter his defensive stance into a ball-you-area pistols stance while straddling the edge of the free-throw-lane line and to anticipate flash-post action from either the low post, the high post, or from anywhere in the weakside perimeter area.

The *low-post* (or, simply, *low*) *call* is the short and quick defensive call made by the back forward or back guard warning the front man of an offensive opponent flashing hard to the ballside block area. The back forward or back guard must also initiate the contact with the cutter to help knock the cutter off of his planned route, to slow him down, and to help destroy the timing of the cutter. The front man must respond by meeting the offensive cutter and making the first contact before then adjusting to the correct fronting stance and position.

The low call is basically the opposite of the empty call in that it warns the front man of an offensive post player flashing to the ballside low-post area. The empty call tells the front man that there is no ballside low-post activity.

The *weakside block area* is the low-post area near the block on the opposite side of the court where the basketball is located (see Area F in Diagram 3.1).

The *ballside elbow area* is the high-post area near the junction of the free-throw-lane line and the free-throw line on the same side the basketball is located (see Area G in Diagram 3.1).

The *open call* is the defensive call made by the back guard telling the up guard that no offensive post player is currently in the ballside high-post area. This call should force the up guard to alter his defensive stance into a ball-you-area pistols stance while straddling the ballside line and to anticipate flash-post action near the high post from any weakside post area or from anywhere in the weakside perimeter area.

The open call also changes the responsibilities of the up guard and the back guard on a reversal pass so that the up guard should step up and defend the ball at the top of the key. This switch in coverage assignments and responsibilities also allows the back guard to help out on the weakside wing area, until the true cover defender (the next ball man) can get there. The call alters the positioning of the back guard so that he can more quickly and easily cover the wing area. On the open call, if no weakside high-post player is approaching, the back guard aligns in the ball-you-area pistols stance at the intersection of the two lines of the free-throw lane that form the tight elbow area. If a weakside high-post player is approaching, the back guard still lines up in the ball-you-area pistols stance, but immediately to the inside and slightly above that offensive player. This location puts the back guard in position so that he can more easily deny the high post the basketball and to also not get pinned in by the high-post player.

The *high-post* (or simply, *high*) *call* is the defensive call made by the back guard warning the up guard that an offensive opponent is flashing hard to the ballside high-post area. The back guard must make physical contact with the offensive cutter to slow him down and also to hopefully bump him off track of his cut. This action also can help destroy the rhythm of the offensive cutter. The up guard must also respond by stepping toward the offensive cutter and making the first contact before then adjusting to the correct fronting stance and position.

The high call is basically the opposite of the open call—where the high call warns of an offensive post player filling the ballside high post, the open call tells the up guard that no ballside offensive post player is approaching.

The *weakside elbow area* is the high-post area near the junction of the free-throw-lane line and the free-throw line on the opposite side of where the basketball is located (see Area H in Diagram 3.1).

The *ballside deep-corner area* is the area on the same side of where the basketball is located—about one full step from the deep baseline just outside of the three-point line (see Area I in Diagram 3.1).

The *weakside deep-corner area* is the area on the opposite side of where the basketball is located—about one full step from the deep baseline just outside of the three-point line (see Area J in Diagram 3.1).

The *ballside short-corner area* is the area one step off of the baseline and halfway between the ballside block and the ballside deep corner (see Area K in Diagram 3.1).

The *ballside wing area* is the area near the free-throw line extended halfway between the free-throw-lane line and the sideline on the side of the floor where the basketball is (see Area L in Diagram 3.1).

The *weakside wing area* is the area near the free throw line extended halfway between the free throw lane line and the sideline on the side of the floor opposite where the basketball is located (see Area M in Diagram 3.1).

The *point area* is the area located at the top of the key and between both sides of the free-throw-lane lines (see Area N in Diagram 3.1).

The *passing line* is the visual concept of an imaginary straight line drawn from where the ball is located to the potential pass receiver in the area that the off-the-ball defender is to be covering (see Diagram 3.2). This concept is identical to the man-to-man defensive concept that should be used in all good man-to-man defenses, using the same passing line. The illustration shows the ball-you-area flat triangle that is partially formed by the passing line (see Diagram 3.2).

The *ball-you-area flat triangle* is the visual concept of an imaginary flat triangle for all off-the-ball defenders describing their positioning with the location of the basketball, themselves, and the offensive man located in the area that they are defending. The three points of the triangle are where the ball is located, where the defender is positioned, and where the offensive opponent in the area to be defended is located. If those three locations are connected by imaginary lines, it should form a flat triangle. The defender should be about one full step off of the imaginary passing line. This concept is almost identical to the man-to-man defensive concept of ball-you-man flat triangle that is a prerequisite of good man-to-man defenses (see Diagram 3.2).

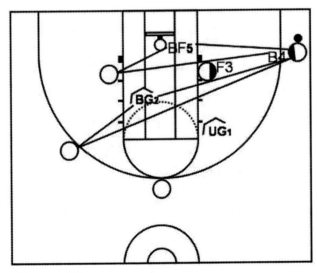

Diagram 3.2

The *short-corner* (or simply, *short*) *call* is the defensive call made by the back forward warning the defense that an offensive opponent has initially set up in (or has cut to) the ballside short-corner area.

The match-up can use various methods to help counter this offensive move when the ball is passed to the player in this dangerous short-corner area. One method that could be used is to have the back forward rotate out on the offensive pass receiver in the short-corner area, while the original ball man rotates down and pushes the original front man out so that he becomes the next back forward. This approach becomes a three-man rotation (see Diagram 6.7). Another method is to treat the pass the same as any other down pass with the down slide using the same personnel (see Diagram 6.5).

Additionally, a third method to help discourage the opposition from passing to the short corner, trap that receiver with the back forward and the original ball man while the original front man remains on the offensive low-post player, but now in a three-quarter front stance (see Diagram 8.8). This defensive stunt will be described in Chapter 8 and, if effectively used, can help convince the offense not to incorporate this pass in its offensive attack very often (see Diagram 8.12).

The fourth method is to utilize another defensive stunt that will be described in detail in Chapter 8. This stunt (called "lock") is to have the back forward again rotate out on the ball and have him stay on the ball indefinitely in a man-to-man defensive scheme. Every other defender must also lock on to the offensive man that is closest to him when the down pass is made to the offensive short corner. This approach places every (so-called "zone") defender into a complete man-to-man defense, using the appropriate man techniques and concepts (see Diagrams 8.19 through 8.22).

The phrase "jump-to-the-ball" describes one of the most important man-to-man defensive techniques, but it can (and should) be one of the most important techniques used in the match-up zone defenses. The phrase simply means that as the ball is being passed by the opposition's offense, all off-the-ball defenders (as well as the ball defender) should quickly jump toward the area where the ball should land. The important key to the technique is that all defenders should not wait until the ball is caught before they react to the new location of the basketball. Doing so makes it easier for the defense to be able to react to what the offense does after the pass is completed, because they are in the proper position more quickly than if they had waited for the pass to be caught.

Jump switch is a defensive technique where the nearest off-the-ball defender switches defensive assignments with the ball defender. This switching can occur whenever an off-the-ball defender is close enough to the ballhandler and can aggressively surprise the opposition's ballhandler. This technique can take place in the multiple match-up zone defense as the offense is being pressured during the dribble as it is utilized in the jump stunt.

Another unexpected opportunity could be whenever the opposition sets a ballscreen for the dribbler. This situation can become a problem for the opposition's offensive player. They might decide not to set screens as part of their offense because the defense is trapping all screens. This approach can also create a more aggressive mindset and attitude for the defense and can influence the defense into being actors and the opposition's offense into the reactors.

Hedging is another defensive technique that is primarily known as a man-to-man defensive technique. It can be used instead of using the switch technique or the jump trapping technique. Like the jump switch technique, hedging can (and should) be incorporated into the multiple match-up zone defensive package. The hedging technique is basically the original defender on the screener actually faking the switch with the original ball defender. The hedging technique can be utilized any time the opposition's offense elects to set ball screens.

4

Terminology of Opponents' Offensive Schemes

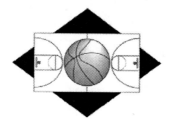

The *wing pass* is an offensive pass from anyone in the point area (01) made to a player in the wing area (02). When the ball is at or above the free-throw line extended, simply say that the ball is high (see Diagram 4.1).

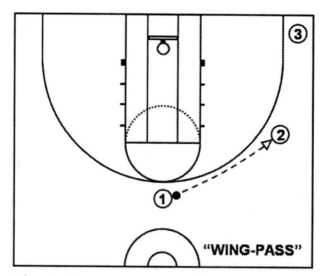

Diagram 4.1

The *down pass* is an offensive pass from a player in the wing area (02) made to a player in the deep-corner area (03). In order for a down pass to be executed, the ball must have first reached the wing area, by way of a wing pass or a wing dribble. When the ball is below the free-throw line extended, use the short phrase the ball is low (see Diagram 4.2).

The *short-corner pass* is an offensive pass from a player in the wing area (03) to a player located in the short-corner area (04). The ball is now low (see Diagram 4.3).

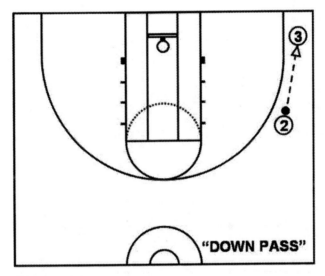

Diagram 4.2

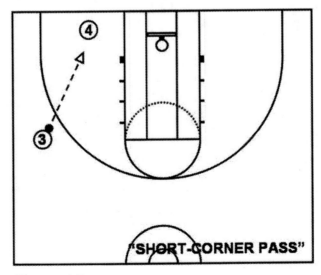

Diagram 4.3

The *up pass* is an offensive pass from a player in the deep-corner area (05) to a player located in the wing area (03). The ball has then gone from low to high (see Diagram 4.4).

The *reversal pass* is an offensive pass made from a player in the wing area (02) to someone in the point area (01). The ball is now high (see Diagram 4.5).

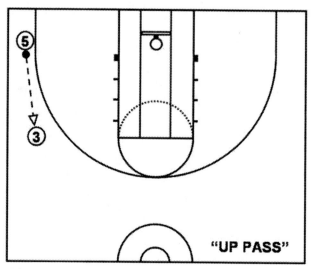

Diagram 4.4

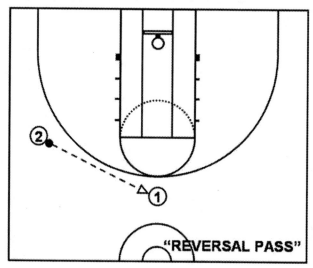

Diagram 4.5

The *skip pass* is an offensive pass made by anyone on one side of the floor (04) to anyone on the perimeter on the opposite side of the floor (03) (see Diagram 4.6), or skipped from 02 to 04 (see Diagram 4.7).

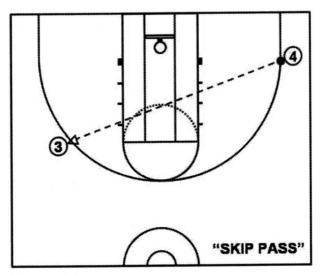

Diagram 4.6

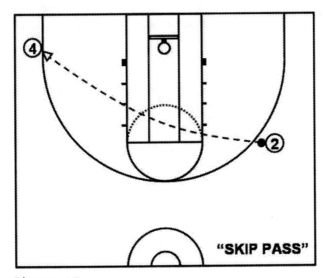

Diagram 4.7

The *low-post pass* is an offensive pass made by a perimeter player (02) anywhere on the perimeter to a post player (05) in the low-post area. This pass is also called an inside pass (see Diagram 4.8).

The *high-post pass* is an offensive pass made by a perimeter player (03) anywhere on the perimeter to a post player (04) in the high-post area (see Diagram 4.9).

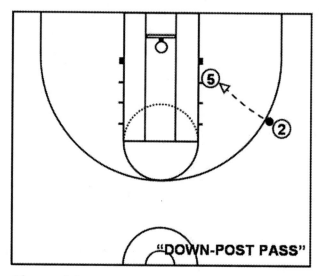

Diagram 4.8

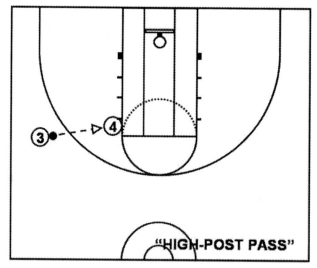

Diagram 4.9

The *wing dribble* is an offensive dribble made by anyone from the point area (01) toward the wing area on either side of the floor. Thus, the ball is high (see Diagram 4.10).

The *down dribble* is an offensive dribble made by an offensive player from the wing area (03) toward the deep-corner area on either side of the floor. Thus, the ball is low (see Diagram 4.11).

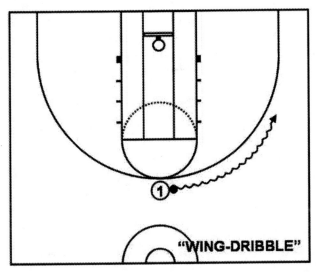

Diagram 4.10

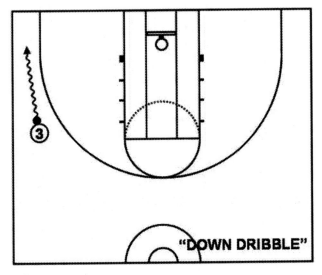

Diagram 4.11

The *up dribble* is an offensive dribble by an offensive player (O3) from the short-corner area (see Diagram 4.12) or deep-corner area out to the wing area (see Diagram 4.13).

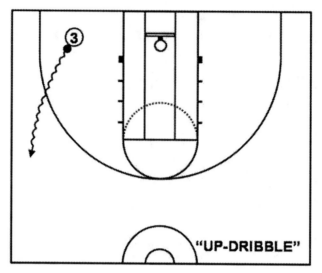

Diagram 4.12

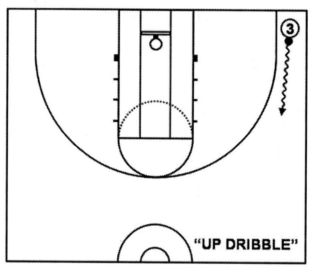

Diagram 4.13

The *reversal dribble* is a dribble by an offensive player (O2) from the wing area that ends up in the point area. This move places the ball high (see Diagram 4.14).

The *pin screen* is an offensive screen set by an offensive player (O5) that would pin a defender in for a cutter (O2) to allow him an open shot. The actual pin-screener (O5) is also a very legitimate threat to the defense and also must be appropriately defended (see Diagram 4.15).

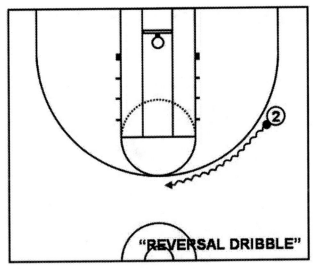

Diagram 4.14

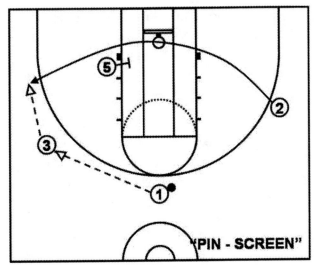

Diagram 4.15

5

Positioning/Location and Required Stances Used by Each Player

Since the 0 zone, the 2 zone, and the 3 zone have very similar initial alignments of their respective defensive personnel, these three match-up zone defenses can be placed in the same basic family. These three different defenses will be discussed as separate entities but within the same grouping. With each defender having different sets of assignments/responsibilities and areas of the floor to cover, each player must be able to handle different positions and locations, regardless of the specific location of the basketball.

Four of these defenders will be off-the-ball defenders (unless a trapping stunt is called) and one defender must always be the ball man. By shading a particular portion of the circle that represents the offensive player, the following diagrams illustrate the actual location in which the ball man will position himself to overplay the ballhandler, or how the front man, the up guard, or the back guard will position himself to front either the offensive low-post or high-post players.

For instance, Diagram 5.1 illustrates a ball man (B3) overplaying the ballhandler to funnel the ball towards the middle of the defense. The shading is on the outside of the offensive ballhandler to demonstrate that the dribbler is to be funneled. The offensive players are represented by the "O," with the ballhandler having the "O" with a dot.

Diagram 5.1 also illustrates the front man (F4) fronting the ballside low-post player in the proper complete frontal location. Additionally, Diagram 5.1 shows an example of the up guard (UG1) fronting the ballside high-post player on the high side of the high-post player (as shown by the shaded area in the diagram) because the ball is high (at or above the free-throw line extended). The up guard straddles the top (or high-side) leg of the offensive player, so the high-post player's high-side leg is between the defender's two legs.

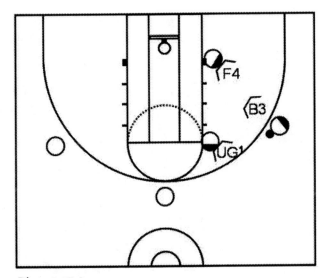

Diagram 5.1

Diagram 5.2 illustrates the new ball man (B4) playing the offensive ballhandler in the deep corner straight up (neither fanning nor funneling the dribbler), with the shading on the ballhandler across the front. The shading on the low-post player in Diagram 5.2 illustrates the new front man (F3) fronting the low-post player straight up. The shading on the high-post player on the bottom portion of the "O" in Diagram 5.2 illustrates the up guard now fronting the high-post player on the bottom half since the ball is below the free-throw line extended.

The shading of the ballhandler on the outside of the "O" in Diagram 5.3 shows an example of the up guard (UG1) on an extended slide positioning himself on the ball to again funnel the ball. Diagram 5.3 also shows the back guard (BG2) now having to front the high post, but doing so only on the top half because the ball is now high (at, or above, the free-throw line extended). F3 fronts the low post (see Diagram 5.3).

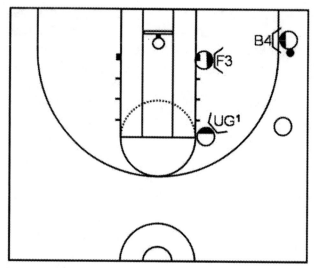

Diagram 5.2

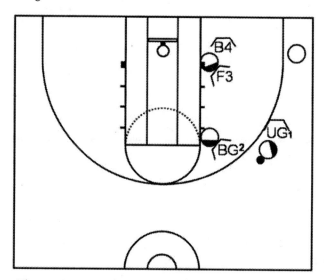

Diagram 5.3

The Ball Man

The ball man is always defending the perimeter player on the ball. This player could be any of the five defenders and it is important to remember that guarding the ball must be done at any spot on the court where the ball is located. The required stance that must be executed by every ball man is called the ball stance.

The ball stance of the ball man is of vital importance to the success of the overall defense. As in all parts of the defense, a great amount of effort, proper location and position, proper stance, and proper techniques are mandatory for defensive success.

Defenders on the ball should utilize three stances. The stance he chooses is dependent upon whether the offensive ballhandler that has the ball has not used his dribble, has already used (and therefore killed) his dribble, or is presently using his dribble.

The first stance is called the ready stance and is used on all ballhandlers that have not used up their dribble. In the multiple match-up zone, the ball man always funnels the basketball towards the middle when the ball is high. In this case, the ball defender's stance should be with the outside foot up (foot closest to the sideline). In Diagram 5.4, the ball man's outside foot is his left foot and that foot should be placed to the outside of and close to touching the dribbler's outside foot (which is the dribbler's right foot), while the inside foot of the defender should be in the direct path of the basket. This alignment should make it extremely difficult for the offensive player to drive toward the sideline.

The defensive footwork and defensive overplay to funnel the ball towards the middle is shown in Diagram 5.4. This defensive overplay positioning of the defender to funnel the dribbler is represented by the shading of the outside portion of the circle in Diagrams 5.1, 5.3, and 5.5.

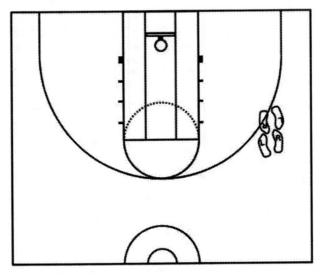

Diagram 5.4

The outside hand of the ball-defender should be up as a way of pressuring the ball to help prevent shots and discouraging passes made to perimeter players towards the sideline. The inside hand also should be extended out in a horizontal manner to help discourage passes toward the middle or the interior. The technique is called tracing the ball, and it should be used often by every ball man defender.

Off-the-ball defenders offer support when the ball man gets beaten on the drive. This backup support should allow the ball man to have confidence in himself and in his teammates so that he can put greater pressure on the ball.

The second stance is called the stick stance and is used by all defenders who are defending the ballhandler who has just killed his dribble. The stick stance is a much more aggressive defensive stance for a defender on the ball. With the dribble killed, one of the three offensive options a ballhandler normally has (dribbling, passing, and shooting) is eliminated. No dribbling threat allows the ball defender to be much more aggressive. The defender should be much closer to the ballhandler and much more aggressive in his actions on the ball. If a defender uses the stick stance correctly and the appropriate techniques on the killed dribbler, the defender should be able to exert maximum defensive pressure on the ballhandler without any threat of being beaten on the dribble. Minimizing the ballhandler's remaining two offensive threats (as a passer and shooter) greatly benefits the defensive team.

The third defensive stance that can be used on the ballhandler is called the dribble stance. The ball man uses this stance on the offensive player when he is actually dribbling the basketball. His arms and hands should be extended laterally to take more space and to help discourage any passing and possible dribble penetration by the ballhandler. Defenders utilizing the dribble stance should have their outside foot staggered higher and close to the dribbler's outside foot. This placement will allow the defender to continue pressuring the dribbler while still influencing the ball towards the middle of the court (where the defense wants the ball to go.) The defender is close enough to the ballhandler to be able to easily and instantly get into the stick stance on a killed dribble and still far enough away to prevent being beaten on dribble drives.

The fourth defensive stance that can used on a ballhandler is a stance that is only used during double-team traps by two defenders. Therefore, the stance is called the trapping stance. It is used only during the two or three possible stunts where traps are involved—the double stunt (with the original ball man and the up guard), the smash stunt (with both the original front man and the ball man), and possibly the jump stunt (with the up guard and the back guard). The smash stunt will be used as the example of showing the proper techniques and concepts of two defenders trapping. The techniques of both trappers can be described with the following phrases:

- No lines-no splits. In this particular instance, no lines means that the original front man cannot give up any baseline drives, while no splits means that the original ball man cannot give up any penetration between the two trappers.
- Both trappers should L-trap with the feet, which means that both trappers position their feet so that they form the letter "L."
- Trace the ball by cross-facing the hands. Both trappers should follow the path of

the ball and when the ball goes over the passer's head, the defenders extend their arms in a cross-armed manner.

- Chest-bump and belly-bump the offensive ballhandler with the chest and stomach. The defenders should put maximum physical pressure on the offensive opponent that has the ball by bumping him with their upper body, but not with their hands or their arms.

- Do not give back any ground surrendered by the ballhandler. When the maximum pressure is placed on the offensive ballhandler and he pivots away from the pressure, the trappers should step toward the ballhandler to place even more pressure on him. This retreating action by the ballhandler to avoid the pressure causes him to lose balance and should eliminate any offensive threats he may possibly have had. The defense should not allow the ballhandler to regain the position he gave up.

- Do not let the offense off of the hook by committing a cheap foul. The defenders should not let the ballhandler get out of the trap by bringing the hands and arms down and hacking the opponent. In the double stunt, the up guard and the ball man are the two defenders that are involved in the double-team trap. The phrase "no lines-no splits" means that the ball man has the nearest sideline to defend, while the up guard is responsible for preventing the penetration between the two trappers. The other concepts and techniques previously discussed remain the same in the double stunt.

These four stances can and should be taught and practiced in breakdown drills such as the stance drills that will be described later. The only exception for the ball man to funnel the ball is when the ball is low and on the baseline. There have the (new) ball man to play the ballhandler straight up and not fan or funnel him. Diagram 5.5

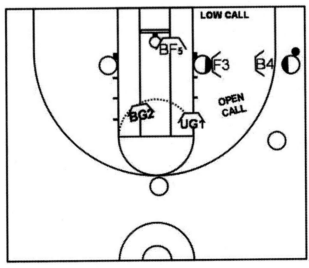

Diagram 5.5

illustrates the ball man (B4) playing the offensive dribbler in a straight up position. If the shading is the front portion of the circle, that defender is playing the ballhandler straight up (as he should when the ball is in the deep corner).

Defensing the Low Post

Complete fronting stance (of the front man) in the front position—used whenever an offensive low-post player is on the ballside block. A low call should be made in this case (see Diagrams 5.5 through 5.16). It should be emphasized repeatedly that a low call and the situation where the ball is low mean two totally different things. A low call means the presence of a ballside low-post player and the phrase "ball is low" means that the location of the ball is anywhere below the free-throw line extended.

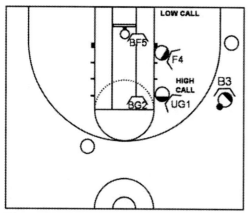

Diagram 5.6

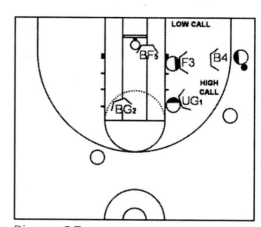

Diagram 5.7

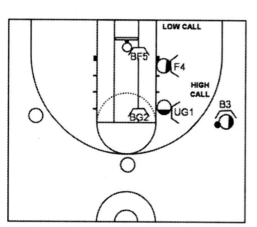

Diagram 5.8

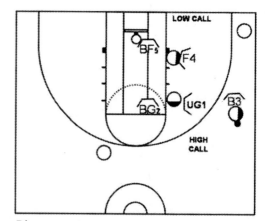

Diagram 5.9

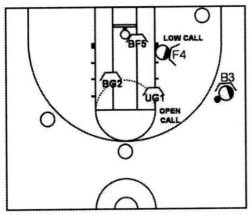

Diagram 5.10

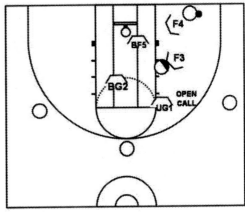

Diagram 5.11

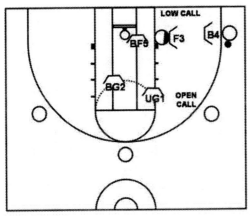

Diagram 5.12

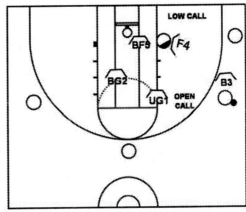

Diagram 5.13

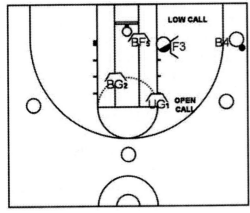

Diagram 5.14

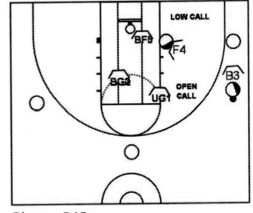

Diagram 5.15

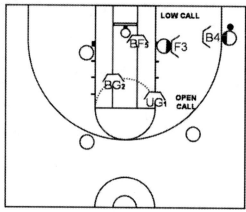

Diagram 5.16

*Pistols stance while straddling the lane line—*used whenever no offensive low-post player is on the ballside block. An empty call should be made in this particular case. The pistols stance prepares the front man for an offensive player to flash to the vacant low post for the ball (see Diagrams 5.17 through 5.21).

In every low call, the front man must always completely front of the ballside low-post player between the post player and the basketball—whether the ball is high or low. He must always make physical contact with the offensive post player and should be in a specific location so that he could make a straight line between the ball (on the perimeter), himself, the offensive post player, and the basket (see Diagrams 5.5 through 5.17).

If the ball is above the free-throw line extended (ball is high), the front man (F4 in Diagram 5.6) should get in the correct position to form the same straight line between the ball and the basket. If the ball is below the free-throw line extended (ball is low), the front man (now F3 in Diagram 5.7) must adjust his fronting location to remain making contact with the post player, to maintain the complete fronting, and to keep the straight line between the ball, himself, the offensive post player, and the basket.

With no ballside low-post player, an empty call should be made. This call should adjust the front man's stance and location to be in a pistols stance at the lane line. This position and stance should allow the front man to be able to defensively front any post player that flashes to the low post (05) as well as to be able to effectively close out on all perimeter players in the corner areas (both short and long) if they receive a down pass (04) (see Diagram 5.21).

*The fronting stance of the front man—*the defensive stance that must be used by any defender who is defending either a low-post player or a high-post player to prevent

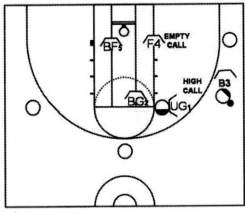

Diagram 5.17

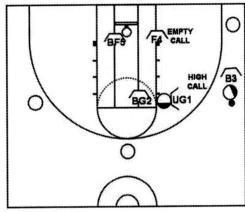

Diagram 5.18

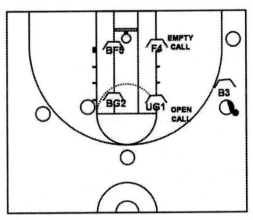

Diagram 5.19

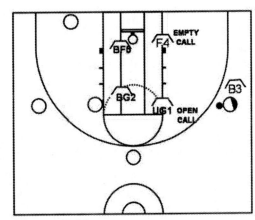

Diagram 5.20

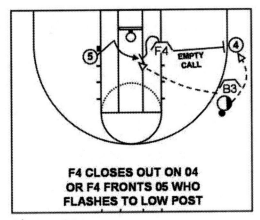

Diagram 5.21

the ball from getting inside against the defense. Tell the post defender to have both of his feet aligned directly in front of both feet of the offensive low-post player. The phrase used for low-post front players is to tell them to "go butt to cup with their hands up." This phrase simply means that the low-post front defenders literally should make contact with the front of the offensive post players. If these post defenders are in a complete fronting stance, with their back and butt making physical contact with the front of the offensive post player, this stance greatly helps restrict the offensive post player from moving, from jumping for a lob pass, or from catching an interior pass from the perimeter. All fronting defenders (for example, F3 in the low post and UG1 in the high post in Diagram 5.7) must keep their hands held straight up to also help discourage the lob pass.

Defensing The High Post

The defensive call "high" means an offensive high-post player is near the ballside elbow area. The defender that is fronting that offensive high-post player should either be the original up guard or the original back guard, depending upon the types of passes previously made before the ball reaches the free-throw line extended or lower. In this case, with the ball at the free-throw line extended after the initial wing pass is made, the up guard (UG1) should front the high-post player in a somewhat different manner than defenders actually front the low post (see Diagram 5.8).

When the ball is at the free-throw line extended (the ball is high), the high-post defender should only straddle the top leg of the offensive high-post player (versus the butt-to-cup stance used in the ballside low-post area by the front man), while still maintaining the same type of physical contact as post defenders do as front men with offensive low-post players. The hands are still held high in the exact manner as the low-post defenders do while fronting the opposition's low-post players.

This stance will give the up guard a position advantage so that he will not get sealed in by the ballside high-post player on a reversal pass from the wing area to the point area. The reversal pass could immediately follow an initial wing pass. The initial wing pass would be defended by the initial ball man (B3) from the backline of the zone and the initial up guard would first cover the ballside high-post area (see Diagram 5.22).

On a reversal pass, the back guard (BG2) must take the pass receiver at the top of the key, so that the up guard can slide around and still front the offensive high post. He originally must be in the proper position and stance to be able to effectively close out on the ball now located at the top of the key. The teaching phrase used is: "If defending the high post, a high call should have been made, then on ball reversal, the (original) up guard becomes the (original) back guard while the (original) back guard becomes the (original) up guard" (see Diagram 5.23).

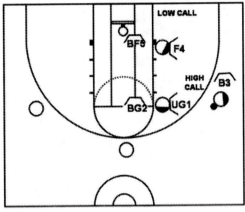

Diagram 5.22

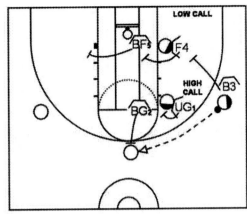

Diagram 5.23

Diagram 5.24 illustrates the scenario when the ball is in the deep corner (ball is low) and a ballside high post (called high) is employed. The ball could have gotten there by an initial wing pass (which causes a wing slide), followed by a down pass (which causes a down slide). The same defender (UG1) should be defending the ballside high-post area. The technique of fronting the ballside high post is different, depending upon whether the ball is above or below the free-throw line extended. The high-post defender should front only the lower half if the ball is low (below the free-throw line extended) (see Diagram 5.24).

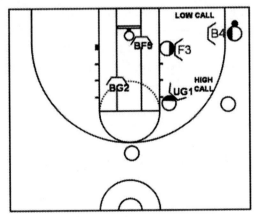

Diagram 5.24

Diagram 5.25 illustrates the scenario when an up pass is made by the offense from the deep corner (03 to 02). This pass dictates that the defense execute an extended slide, which extends the up guard (UG1) out on the ball and the back guard (BG2) to extend over to front the high post on the high side. The back guard should do so by only fronting the top half of the post player, since the ball is high (near or above the free-throw line extended) (see Diagram 5.25).

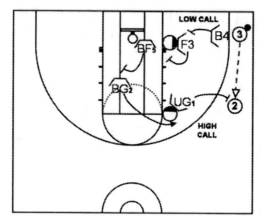

Diagram 5.25

With no ballside high post, the back guard (BG2) calls open, which allows the original up guard (UG1) to align in a ball-you-area pistols stance at the ballside elbow area on the initial wing pass. On the subsequent reversal pass, since UG1 is not defending a ballside high post, he is the designated defender that should come up and out to defend the area at the top of the key (and not the original BG2). Therefore, the phrase used to help teach in this scenario is: "If the open call is made (signifying that the ballside high post is vacant), the up guard remains as the up guard and the back guard stays as the back guard when the ball is reversed." This approach allows BG2 to drop into the lane towards the dotted circle and to straddle the manside line and help to bump potential high-post flashers and also to be able to help on the coverage of the wing pass after the reversal pass is made. This action occurs because the up guard (UG1) takes the man who receives the reversal pass at the top of the key (see Diagram 5.26).

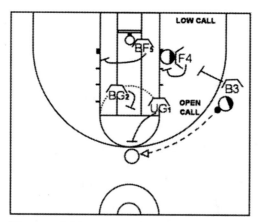

Diagram 5.26

An empty call signifies that no low-post player is on the ballside. Therefore, the front man (F4 in Diagram 5.27) must be in a ball-you-area pistols stance and straddle the lane line. This positioning gives him time to react to a low-post flash cut to the block and also puts him in position to be able to successfully close out on the perimeter shooter in the deep corner, while executing a down slide after the offense makes a down pass (see Diagram 5.28).

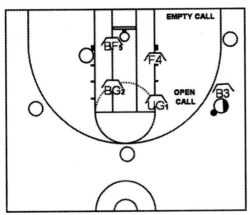

Diagram 5.27

Diagram 5.28

After this down slide, a new ball man (B4 in Diagram 5.29) and a new front man (F3 in Diagram 5.29) are in the same ball-you-area pistols stance and in the same lane line position/location as the original front man. Notice that the new front man (F3) has not changed the fronting position, even though the location of the ball has changed from high to low.

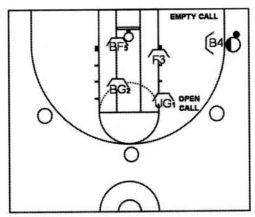

Diagram 5.29

Attacker in Both Low and High Post

In an offensive set that has both a high post (a high call) and a low post on the ballside (a low call), the front man maintains the complete fronting position between the ball, the low-post player, and the basket. The location of the ball above or below the free-throw line extended makes only a slight difference to the front man in staying between the ball, the post player, and the basket (see F4 in Diagram 5.30 and F3 in Diagram 5.31).

The location of the ball dictates either the high half or the lower half of only the high-post player that is fronted by the defender (either the up guard or the back guard) that is defending him because the ball is at or above the free-throw line extended (the ball is high) (see Diagram 5.30). Diagram 5.31 illustrates that the ball is below the free-throw line extended (the ball is low) and therefore the offensive high post should be fronted on the lower half (see Diagram 5.31).

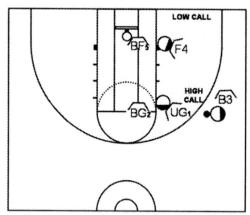

Diagram 5.30

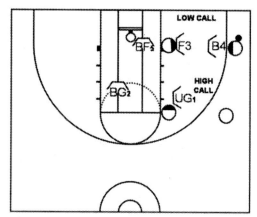

Diagram 5.31

Off-the-Ball Defense

The off-the-ball ball-you-area pistols stance—the stance that should be used by any player when he is defending an area away from the ball and/or when he is not guarding either an offensive high-post or low-post player. These defenders are sitting in a stance with their feet shoulder-width apart, and the ballside foot slightly ahead of the opposite foot.

The hands are clenched in fists, with index fingers of both hands (similar to two pistols) pointing in two opposite directions. One index finger is pointing toward the basketball while the other index finger should be pointing to the off-the-ball area that is being defended by that particular defender.

The location for each defender is determined by the assignment or responsibility of that specific defender and also the location of the ball (high or low). Examples of the defensive stances and the positioning of the two off-the-ball defenders that are in the pistols stances (BG2 and BF5) are shown in Diagram 5.32.

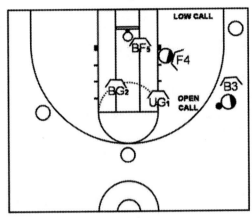

Diagram 5.32

In Diagram 5.32, a change in responsibilities (and therefore in the positioning and location of BG2) would result if a wing pass and a high-post call (not an open call) were made. If an offensive player was at the high post that was defended by UG1 and the ball was at the free-throw line extended and defended by B3, BG2 would need to straddle the ballside line and not the manside line, because of his lob support that must be given to UG1 at the high post. BG2 must be up the ballside line at the free-throw line extended and not lower than the free-throw line so that he can successfully execute the centered-up slide at the top of the key after a reverse pass. He must be able to stop the shot at the top of the key after the reverse pass and become the new up guard, because the original up guard is occupied with the offensive high-post player.

Without that offensive high-post player, UG1 would remain as the up guard, which would allow the back guard to remain as the back guard. And BG2 would stay lower in the lane to clog up the middle for flash post players, since he would not have to take the receiver of the reverse pass at the top of the key.

The defensive stances and positioning of both the front man (F4) and the up guard (UG1) are also illustrated in Diagram 5.32, which uses a low call and an open call when the ball is on the defense's left side of the floor and with the ball at or above the free-throw line extended. Diagram 5.33 shows the same offensive post positioning scenario, but now with the ball located below the free-throw line extended. Notice that BG2 now is settled slightly lower into the lane (less than a full step) for two reasons: the ball is in the deep corner and he does not have to provide lob support for UG1, and also because no ballside high-post player is being employed (open call).

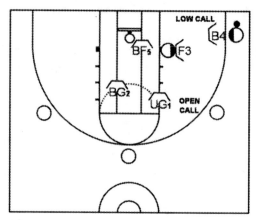

Diagram 5.33

After the down pass, which caused the defense to execute a down slide, a new ball man (B4) and a new front man (F3) are now in position. The back forward (BF5) remains the same player, his stance stays the same, and his positioning/location remains at the same ballside line. The back guard also remains the same player, as does his stance and positioning because he started at the manside line and near the dotted circle (due to an open call) and remains at the manside line and the dotted-circle area (because the ball is down in the deep corner). The up guard stays as the up guard and keeps the same pistols stance and positioning (at the ballside elbow-lane line) since the ball is now below the free-throw line extended.

Coaches should constantly tell these off-the-ball defenders (that are not fronting) to keep their head on a swivel, so that they can constantly and quickly turn their head to maintain vision of the basketball as well as the area they are defending at all times.

Off-the-ball defenders must always see the ball and the man in their area. Diagram 5.34 illustrates the stances and locations of all five defenders with the ball this time on the defense's right side of the court at the free-throw line extended and with the ball being low (below the free-throw line extended).

The offensive post situation is also different, with only a high-post player positioned on the ballside, which means an empty call for the vacant low-post area and a high call for the offensive high post should have been made. This pistols stance should always be used by the back forward (BF3) and the back guard (BG2) on the weakside of the defense. The back guard should be located at the manside line and the dotted-circle area for the same two reasons: open call situation, and the ball is low in the deep corner. This stance should also be used by the ballside front man (F4) only if an empty call is used (no ballside low-post opponent), as is the case in Diagram 5.34.

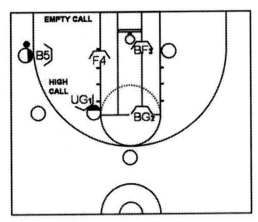

Diagram 5.34

If the ball was at the free-throw line extended after a wing pass and a ballside high-post player was used, the back guard would have to be at the ballside line and also on the free-throw line so that, on a reverse pass, the back guard would be able to close out on the reverse-pass receiver. The empty call dictates in this case that the front man uses the same ball-you-area pistols stance with the same head on a swivel technique.

The only other situation that would necessitate that the ball-you-area pistols stance be used by another defender could be by the up guard (UG1) if no ballside high-post opponent is present, which would be declared by an open call made by the back guard (BG2) (see Diagram 5.35).

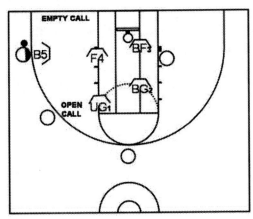

Diagram 5.35

The Back Forward

The back forward must always be in a ball-you-area pistols stance and his location/position should always be straddling either the ballside line or the manside line and always forming a ball-you-area flat triangle.

Pistols stance at the block level while straddling the manside line—used whenever an empty call is employed, regardless of whether the ball is high or the ball is low. This simply means that the back forward is at the manside line (MSL) whenever an empty call is made (which means no offensive low-post player is on the ballside block) (see Diagrams 5.17 through 5.20, 5.27, 5.34, and 5.35).

Pistols stance at the block level while straddling the ballside line—used whenever a low call is made, regardless of the location of the basketball. In other words, the back forward is at the ballside line (BSL) only if an offensive low-post player is on the ballside block. A low call must always be made whenever an offensive post player is on the ballside (see Diagrams 5.5 through 5.16, 5.22 through 5.26, and 5.28 through 5.33).

Whenever the offense has dictated to the defense to be in a low call (with an offensive post player near the ballside low- or mid-post area), regardless of the location of the ball, the back forward should be in a pistols stance straddling the ballside line.

Simply stated, the back forward should always be in the proper stance and position/location and then use the proper techniques to accomplish his two primary responsibilities. The back forward's first priority is to prevent the lob pass to a ballside low-post opponent. To perform this task, he must be in the correct pistols stance and be straddling the correct ballside line to help defend against the lob pass.

His second main defensive priority is to be able to effectively close out on a perimeter player on his side of the floor at the free-throw line extended if the ball is swung from the original ballside to his side of the floor. This slide can be done more effectively by getting to that area as quickly as possible. Being in the proper stance, straddling the manside line, and then using the proper techniques of closing out on the ball and pressuring the basketball can help the player get to that designated area more quickly.

The Back Guard

Pistols stance at the dotted-circle level while straddling the manside line—used by the back guard on all open calls, regardless of the location of the ball and only on high calls (which means a ballside high-post player) and only with the ball being low (below the free-throw line extended). Thus, whenever no offensive high-post player is on the ballside elbow (open call), regardless of whether the ball is above or below the free-throw line extended, the back guard should be at the dotted-circle area, straddling the manside line (see Diagrams 5.5, 5.10 through 5.16, 5.19, 5.20, 5.26, 5.28, 5.29, 5.32, 5.33, and 5.35).

The same pistols stance should also be used at the ballside line and at the actual free-throw line (instead of at the dotted-circle level) when an offensive post player is at the ballside high-post area (high call) and when the ball is at or above the free-throw line extended (the ball is high) (see Diagrams 5.6, 5.8, 5.9, 5.17, 5.18, 5.22, 5.23, and 5.30). But when a high call (ballside high-post player) is made and the ball is low (i.e., below the free-throw line extended), the back guard should straddle the manside line (MSL) at the dotted-circle area, because he will have enough time to effectively close out on the reverse pass after the up pass is made (see Diagrams 5.7, 5.24, 5.25, 5.31, and 5.34).

Pistols stance at the free throw shooting line, while straddling the ballside line— used whenever the ball is high and a high call is made. In other words, both conditions must apply—the ball at the free-throw line extended and an offensive post player at the ballside high-post area. A high call should be made in this particular case to warn defenders that a ballside high-post player is being employed (see Diagrams 5.6, 5.8, 5.9, 5.17, 5.18, 5.22, 5.23, and 5.30.)

Front stance while straddling the top half of the post player at the high post— used should be a high call made and only after the up guard has made his extended slide out on the ball, which then extends the back guard to the occupied high-post area. On the extended slide and with a high call, the back guard must make an extended slide and end up on the high side of the ballside high-post player as the original up guard has extended out to the ballhandler at the free-throw line extended (after the up pass was made from the deep corner). If the ball is then reversed, the original back guard must then take the ballhandler at the top of the key and the up guard must then slide back in to defend the ballside high-post player (see Diagrams 5.25 and 5.38).

The Up Guard

Front stance while straddling the one half of the post player at the high post— used based upon the location of the ball. A high call should be made every time an offensive post player is near the ballside high-post area and the up guard should straddle one half of that ballside high-post player, dependent upon whether the ball is low or high. If the ball is low (below the free-throw line extended), the up guard should straddle the lower half of the offensive post player (see Diagrams 5.2, 5.7, 5.24, 5.25, 5.31, and 5.34). The up guard should straddle the top half of the offensive post player when the ball is high (at or above the free-throw line extended) (see Diagrams 5.6, 5.8, 5.9, 5.17, 5.18, 5.22, 5.23, and 5.30).

Pistols stance toward the ball at the ballside elbow— used whenever no offensive high-post player is on the ballside elbow. An open call should be made in this particular case (see Diagrams 5.5, 5.10 through 5.16, 5.19 through 5.21, 5.26 through 5.29, 5.32, 5.33, 5.35, and 5.36).

Ball-man stance funneling the ball—utilized whenever the ball is up-passed from the corner to the offensive wing player near the free-throw line extended, where the ball is high. This actual extended slide should be executed by the original ball man, the up guard, and the back guard (see Diagrams 5.3 and 5.25).

Ball-man stance playing the offensive ballhandler straight up—used when a reversal pass is made out to the top of the key and when no offensive high-post player is employed (which should be declared with an open call). The original up guard remains the up guard, and the back guard remains in his original position (see Diagram 5.26).

Stunts

Trap stance—used by the two defenders who are trapping the ball. The jump stunt is not technically a trapping stunt, but more of a jump-switch between the two defenders, so the trapping techniques are not used in this stunt. The jump stunt is activated by the opposition dribbling the ball, and the smash and the double stunts are activated by a specific pass.

The two defenders involved in the jump stunt are the up guard and the back guard, but the smash stunt and the double stunt are the two stunts where double-team traps are utilized at two different locations on the court. The smash stunt takes place in the deep corner after the offense makes a down pass and the double stunt takes place at the free-throw line extended after a wing pass is made.

The two trappers would be the original ball man and front man in the smash stunt or the original ball man and the up guard in the double stunt. The trapping techniques used by both stunts are basically the same, just in different locations and by different players.

The smash stunt is activated by the down pass, with a wing pass preceding it. The original ball man (B3) must approach under control the pass receiver in the deep corner with an inside-out angle on his closeout. The original front man (F4) must approach the ball under control from the low-post area and be squared up on the baseline in the same manner as he does in his down slide (after the down pass). What is different is that the original front man (F4) has double-team help from the original ball man (B3).

F4 has the no lines part and B3 has the no split part of the trapping technique. Both execute the other techniques previously discussed. The original back forward

(BF5) must again come around on the baseline side of the offensive low post to three-quarter front the post (as he does on the typical down slide). Instead of releasing the coverage when the original ball man (B3) makes his down slide in the base defense, the (original) back forward remains there to three-quarter front the offensive post. Obviously, the smash stunt can be executed on either side of the floor (see Diagram 5.36).

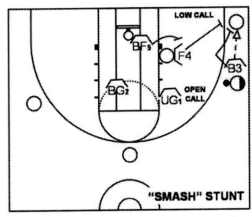

Diagram 5.36

The double stunt is activated only by the wing pass to the free-throw line extended. It first appears that this typical wing slide follows the initial wing pass. The first ball man (B3) closes out on the ball in the same manner as he does when executing his wing slide. What is different is that he will receive double-team help from the original up guard (UG1) who will follow the wing pass and trap with the ball man (L3). The original ball man (B3) has the no lines part and the original up guard (UG1) has the no splits part of the first technique.

All of the other trapping techniques are followed by the trappers. The original back guard (BG2) must then cover the ballside high-post area if a high call is made (see Diagram 5.37). If an open call is made, the original back guard must be conscious that the up guard obviously cannot defend that ballside high-post area, but he must remember that he still is the back guard and must execute the centered-up slide if and when the ball is reversed out of the trap to the top of the key (see Diagram 5.38).

Intercept stance—the defensive stance that the up guard (UG1 in Diagram 5.39) should use when the ball is in the deep or the short corner on either the smash stunt or the choke stunt (see Diagram 8.16). The stance is not a ball-you-area pistols stance, but a new and unique area-you-area pistols stance used by the up guard. In this instance, the defender's back is not facing the baseline, but instead is facing the offensive player with the basketball, while pointing to the ballside high-post area and the wing area at the free-throw line extended. This position and stance allows the up

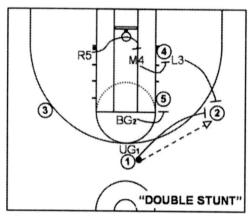

Diagram 5.37

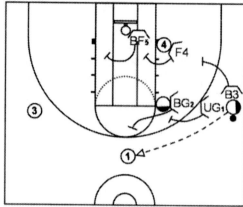

Diagram 5.38

guard to be able to read the passer's eyes while still pointing to the ballside high-post area and also the ballside wing area. When the ball is immediately passed, the up guard should use a front-crossover step and then use the man-to-man defensive technique of the long arm to go for the interception. This technique helps the defender avoid contact with the offensive pass receiver while still going for the interception (see Diagram 5.39).

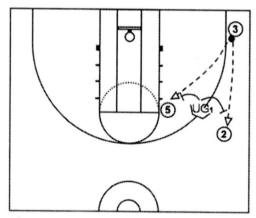

Diagram 5.39

The up guard (UG1) is in the defensive intercept stance facing the offensive player (03) in the deep corner. He is pointing his left index finger towards 05 at the high post and pointing his right index finger at 02 at the ballside wing area. If 03 looks to pass the ball to 05 (on the up guard's left), the UG1 should make his first step with his right foot in a front crossover and make his right arm the immediate long arm and go for the interception. If 03 looks to pass the ball to 02 (on the up guard's right), the UG1 should make his first step with his left foot in a front crossover and make his left arm the new long arm and go for the interception. Anytime the long arm technique is used, the defender should look down the long arm to be able to see both the offensive pass receiver and the ball in flight. If no turnovers result from the up pass, all the defenders in the match-up should be in the proper stances and locations shown in Diagram 5.40.

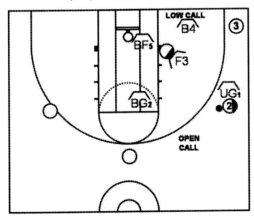

Diagram 5.40

Positioning and Locations with Proper Stances of Match-Up Zone Defenders		
Front Man		
Empty Call (No low-post player) **Low Call**	If ball is high or low If ball is high or low	Pistols stance on lane line Fronting stance on low-post player
Back Forward		
Empty Call (No low-post player) **Low Call**	If ball is high or low If ball is high or low	Pistols stance on manside line Pistols stance on ballside line
Back Guard		
Open Call (No high-post player)	If ball is high or low	Pistols stance on manside line near the dotted-circle area
High Call	Only if ball is low	Pistols stance on manside line near the dotted-circle area
High Call	Only if ball is high	Pistols stance on ballside line at the free-throw line
Up Guard		
Open Call (No high-post player) **High Call**	If ball is low or high Only if ball is low	Pistols stance on ballside elbow lane line Fronting stance on lower half of ballside high-post player
High Call	Only if ball is high	Fronting stance" on top half of ballside high-post player

Figure 5.1

59

6

Slides

With three different initial alignments in which the match-up zone can start, each initial alignment initiates a separate defense in itself. Each defense must have its own defensive slides and its own various responsibilities and assignments for specific players. Part of the responsibilities would include the stances and individual player positions when the ball is located at various spots on the floor.

But the initial personnel alignments have certain similarities (and therefore, the assignments/responsibilities as well as the locations/positions of individual defensive players have similarities as well). To prevent repeating each defensive slide and the other responsibilities, the three match-up zone defenses can be grouped into one category. In this group, both the 0 zone and the 2 zone have three initial backline defenders, called the left man (X3), the middle man (X4), and the right man (X5).

The two front-line defenders are positioned in slightly different alignments, which gives the defenses different cosmetic appearances. The only difference between the 0 zone and the 2 zone is the initial placement of the up guard (X1) and the back guard (X2). In the 0 zone, the up guard and the back guard are set up in a vertical tandem (see Diagram 6.1), while in the 2 zone, they could be described as being in a horizontal tandem (see Diagram 6.2).

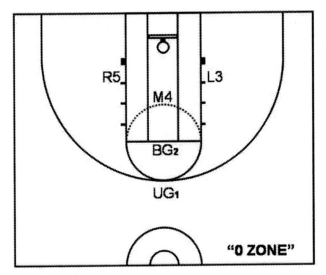

Diagram 6.1

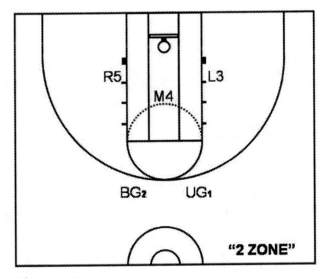

Diagram 6.2

In the 3 zone, the left man and the right man initially start up in the second line (of the three lines) of the defense. The 3 zone is very similar to the 0 zone, with the exception being that the left man (X3) and the right man (X5) have walked themselves up to the free-throw line extended (see Diagram 6.3). The middle man (X4) remains in the same location in all three of these zone defenses (see Diagrams 6.1 through 6.3).

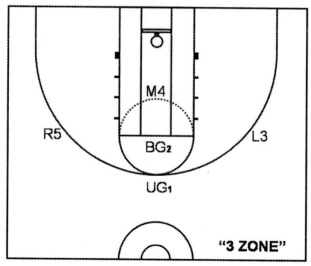

Diagram 6.3

With the different alignments also come different responsibilities and different names for the defensive personnel. Still, to enable a coaching staff to effectively teach more than one match-up zone, much of the terminology, responsibilities, and techniques should be very similar. Otherwise, it would be extremely difficult for a team to successfully grasp the finer points of each match-up defense. This chapter will provide the basic definitions and coverage responsibilities for the general slides of all three specific match-up zone defenses, using the 0 zone alignment in all the diagrams.

The *general wing slide* takes place only after the wing pass, which is a pass from the top of the zone offense to an offensive player located near the free-throw line extended. In general, the defender that is closest to that specific wing area where the ball is passed will slide to that area and become the new ball man (B3) to defend the ballhandler. In this example, since many offenses are right-handed, the offense will make a wing pass to their right side; which is the defense's left side (see Diagram 6.4). The new ball man (B3) will attempt to funnel the ballhandler towards the middle, to also prevent the ballhandler from driving in a direct line to the basket, from taking uncontested and un-pressured shots, and also from making easy passes especially to their offensive post players.

Each defense will have slight variations of the wing slide, but basically this slide is the same in all three match-up zone defenses. The remaining defenders will become the front man (F4), another the back forward (BF5), another the up guard (UG1), and another the back guard (BG2) (see Diagram 6.4).

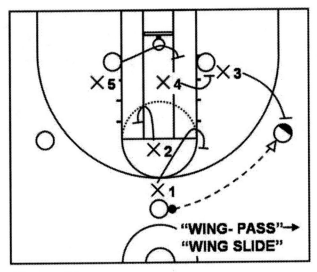

Diagram 6.4

The *general down slide* is a reaction to the down pass from the wing area to an offensive player in the deep-corner area. It involves three defensive players so that the low-post area remains protected and the new player with the ball is instantly and completely defended.

The initial ball man (B3) on the ball makes a cut to the ballside low post, while the first front man (F4) closes out on the new ballhandler quickly (but under control) to become the next ball man. The momentary lack of complete coverage of the low post is protected by the original back forward (BF5) coming around to three-quarter front the low post—always from the baseline side of the offensive post—until the original ball man (X3) gets there to become the new front man and front the post. The up guard (UG1) and the back guard (BG2) basically remain in their assigned areas. Each defense will have slight variations of the down slide, but basically this slide is the same in the 0 zone, the 2 zone, and the 3 zone (see Diagrams 6.5 and 6.6).

The *general short-corner slide* is a simple reaction to the offense's pass to the short corner. Most offenses that have a player either start or end up in this short-corner area also have a post player near the ballside block area. The short-corner call must be made by the back forward to alert the defense, particularly the front man and the ball man.

The first defensive option is the three-man rotation between the back forward, the front man, and the ball man The back forward (BF5) should be in the proper pistols stance straddling the ballside line (whenever an offensive post player is on the ballside

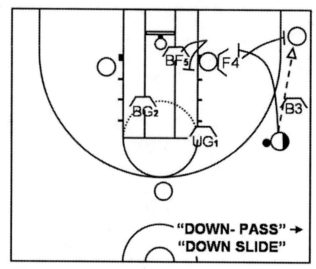

Diagram 6.5

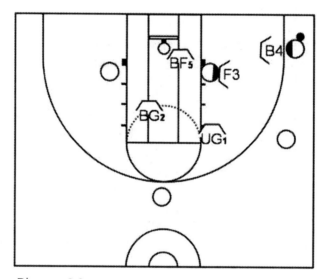

Diagram 6.6

block). Doing so should allow him to adequately cover the pass down to the offensive player in the short corner. When the pass is made, the back forward should be able to quickly close out on the ball and take away the baseline drive, as well as discourage the quick jumper or the touch pass to the ballside low-post player, with the short corner covered (by BF5). The front man (F4) must remain in a position directly between the ball and the low-post player. He will remain there until the original ball man (B3) pushes him out. Therefore, the original front man (F4) becomes the new back forward while the original ball man becomes the new front man.

The new ball man on the offensive player in the short corner is now B5. This tactic is one of the most dangerous types of offensive action that the opponents can execute because the player in the short corner is so close to the basket. But with proper slides from all three backline defenders, this offensive movement can be contained (see Diagram 6.7).

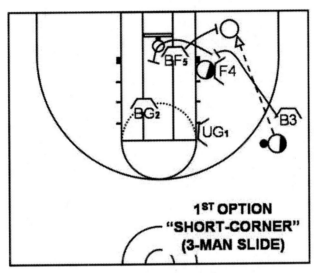

Diagram 6.7

The second option could be the two-man rotation between the front man (F4) and the ball man (B3). After the call has been made and the ball has been passed to the offensive opponent in the short corner, the front man (F4) must close out on the ball in the short corner and immediately take away the baseline drive and the short jump shot. The back forward (BF5) must rotate over to help out if the offensive short-corner player drives the baseline. He must also momentarily help on the offensive post player on the ballside block until the original ball man (B3) rotates down to become the new front man and front the ballside low post. The original back forward then goes back to remain as the back forward (see Diagram 6.8).

Another possible option that the defense could possibly use to counter the pass to the short corner is for the defense to trap the ball on the baseline. The original back forward (BF5) quickly closes out on the offensive player that caught the ball in the short corner (04), while the original front man (F4) adjusts his position but remains fronting the low post (05) as the front man. The original ball man (B3) reacts to the pass and quickly traps the ball in the short corner. The original up guard rotates over and splits the difference between the two perimeter players, anticipating a quick escape pass out of the trap to either of the two closest potential pass receivers (01 and 02). With the offense having players at the ballside wing, the ballside post, and the ballside short corner, there must likely would never be a ballside high-post player (see Diagram 6.9).

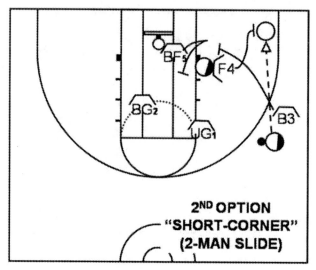

Diagram 6.8

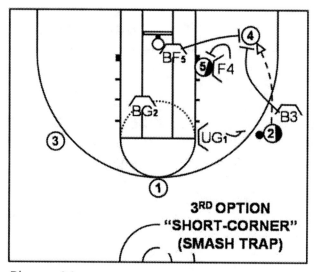

Diagram 6.9

A fourth option that can be utilized is one of the defensive stunts that could be used in other scenarios. This stunt can be used to possibly discourage offensive opponents from using the short-corner scheme. Again, as soon as an offensive player is in the short-corner area, the short corner call must be made by the back forward (BF5). When the pass is made to O4 in the short corner, the original back forward again closes out on the ball and then remains on O4 in the short corner (as he would in the first and the third options previously mentioned). The original front man (F4) still fronts O5 at the low post, but the original ball man (B3) remains matched up on the original passer (02). Both the up guard (UG1) and the back guard (BG2) search for an open offensive player and then match up on that particular player (BG2 on 03, and UG1 on 01). All five players are now matched up on specific players and all five remain in a man-to-man defensive scheme. This alignment can cause great confusion with the offense attacking a man defense with a zone offense (see Diagram 6.10). Depending on the abilities of your personnel, you might not want to teach the short-corner trap and the smash stunt in the same year. The short-corner trap and the smash stunt have a slightly different slides and responsibilities. But you definitely want to teach the lock stunt along with either the smash stunt or the short-corner trap.

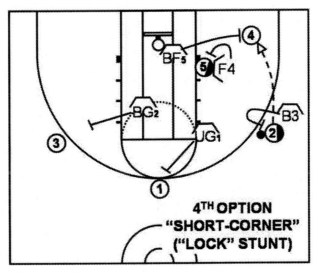

Diagram 6.10

The *general extended slide* is the reaction to the up pass that both the up guard and the back guard must make to cover the ballside wing and the possible ballside high post when the ball is up-passed from the deep or short corner on the ballside. The up guard (UG1) extends out to pressure the offensive wing that just received the up pass (02), while the back guard (BG2) also slides over to now cover the ballside high post in order to cover any offensive post player (on the top half). If no high-post player is utilized (empty call), he should remain in the pistols stance and go to the ballside line.

The latest ball man (B4) drops inside toward the offensive post player (04) along the baseline. Doing so will help discourage a lob pass from the top of the key (01) to the offensive baseline corner player (04) that runs along the baseline toward the basket. B4 makes sure that he takes away the lob route but also makes sure that he does not get inside the offensive post player to keep from getting pin-screened. The ball man (B4) that covers the deep corner on the original down pass must cover the corner area again if a second down pass occurs. If the scenario is open (no ballside high post), the back guard (BG2) can move over only to the ballside because he is the defender who must cover the player at the top of the key that receives the reversal pass (01) (see Diagram 6.11).

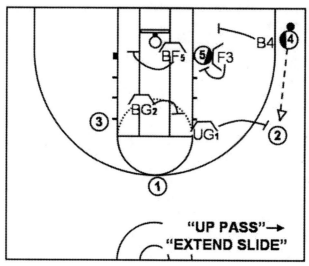

Diagram 6.11

The *general centered-up slide* is predicated upon the reversal pass. This reversal pass (from 02 to 01) could have been preceded by the up pass (from 04 to 02) from the ballside corner area, which means that an extend slide had to have first taken place (Diagram 6.11 illustrates the up pass). In this case, both the up guard (UG1) and the back guard (BG2) had to have extended toward the ballside wing on the up pass (from 04 to 02).

This centered-up slide involves both the up guard (UG1) and the back guard (BG2). After an extend slide takes place, the back guard (BG2) must take the offensive point-guard area on the reversal pass because the up guard (UG1) had extended out on the ball at the wing area after the up pass (see Diagram 6.11). If the initial back guard (BG2) becomes the new up guard, this situation would force the initial up guard (UG1) to become the new back guard (see Diagrams 6.12 and 6.13). X2 in Diagram 6.13 is the BG2 in Diagram 6.12, and X1 in Diagram 6.13 is the UG1 in Diagram 6.12. You should also note that the back line now has X3 (B3) and X4 (F4) exchanging positions and duties. This alignment is the basic slide of all three match-up zones.

The second offensive scenario would be if the reversal pass (from 02 to 01) is made following a wing pass (from 01 to 02), with no up pass having taken place (in

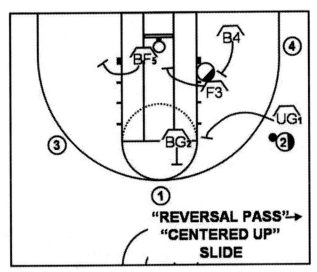

Diagram 6.12

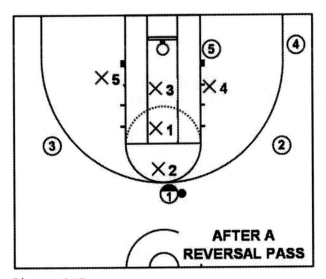

Diagram 6.13

other words, no pass having been made to the corner). In this case, the up guard and the back guard have not extended out on the ball on the extended slide, when the ball is on the wing. If the scenario is thus, and the up guard (UG1) is in an open situation (and has no ballside high post coverage), it is sometimes better for the up guard to take the receiver at the top of the key who catches the reversal pass (01). Doing so allows the initial back guard (BG2) to remain as the back guard (see Diagram 6.14).

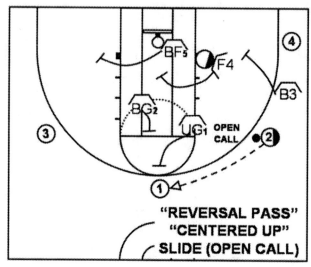

Diagram 6.14

Diagram 6.15 shows if a wing pass (to 02 from 01) was initially made (and no down pass was made) and the offense has a ballside high-post player (05) in position (a high call), the UG1 must semi-front that player on the top half in that area while the back guard is in a ball-you-area pistols stance at the ballside line, near the dotted circle. On this particular reversal pass, the center-up slide must be executed with the original back guard (BG2) stepping out on the ball at the top of the key, while the original up guard (UG1) must come around to cover the high post and then remain as the new back guard (see Diagram 6.15).

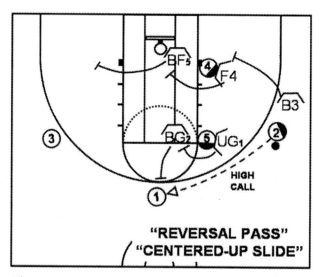

Diagram 6.15

The *general switch slide* is predicated upon the wing dribble. When the up guard picks up the offensive point guard (O1) dribbling the ball in the front court and the dribbler continues dribbling the ball to the free-throw line extended, that up guard keeps constant pressure on the dribbler until the first ball man (B3) comes out to pick up the dribbler and yells "Switch!" If a high-post player is utilized (which requires a high call), this switch slide then tells the up guard (UG1) to back off and to become the new back guard. The reason is that the initial back guard (BG2) covers the offensive player at the ballside high post and he remains there to semi-front that offensive player on the top half, becoming the new up guard (UG2) (see Diagram 6.16).

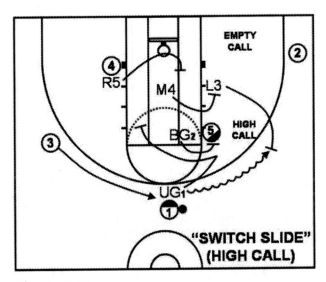

Diagram 6.16

If no high post is used, an open call should be made, and the UG1 will remain as the up guard. After the switch slide by B3 (and an open call), the UG1 should get in a pistols stance at the ballside line so that he can effectively cover the top of the key, if an immediate reversal pass is made by the offense (from O1 to O3). Doing so allows BG2 to remain as the back guard on the reversal pass and help out on the wing pass on the left side of the floor, while UG1 takes the pass receiver (O3) at the top of key (see Diagram 6.17).

The *general skip-pass slide* is predicated upon the skip pass. The skip pass rule is a basic rule that simply states the closest and quickest defender to the ball should take the receiver that caught the skip pass. It does not matter who gets there, as long as a defender gets there quickly. The defender should rush out as quickly as possible and prevent the three-point shot, knowing that he has support behind him against dribbling penetration. His top priority is to prevent the three-point shot, or at least make it a contested shot.

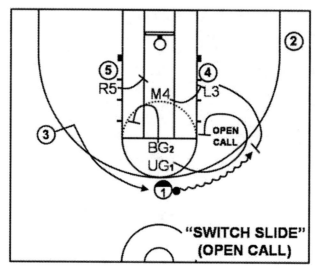

Diagram 6.17

If the quickest player to get there prevents the shot and then the proper player gets there, the proper player then switches off to bump the first defender back to his normal position. Simply put, a skip pass causes the defense to scramble and, when done successfully to prevent the shot, all players should then get back to their correct coverage areas. Diagram 6.18 shows the scramble routes of the skip-pass slide on a pass from the ballside deep corner (04) to the weakside wing area (03). Diagram 6.19 shows the personnel placement after defenders have adjusted their coverage. When the proper defender gets to the skip pass receiver, he yells "No shot! No shot!" to tell the original (closest to man) defender to back off.

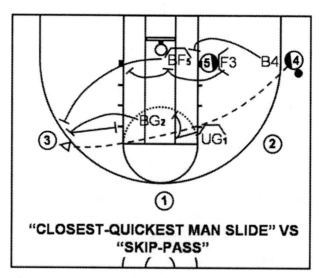

Diagram 6.18

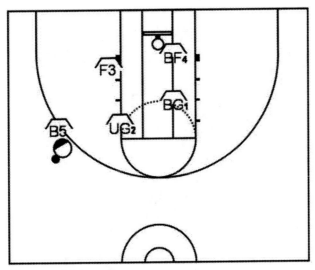

Diagram 6.19

Diagrams 6.20 and 6.21 show the scramble routes of the skip-pass slide on a pass from the ballside wing (O2) to the weakside deep corner (O3) followed by coverage placement with the correct personnel. You want X5 to cover both skip passes when possible. After X5 arrives, BG2 (X2) should drop back to his original coverage positioning.

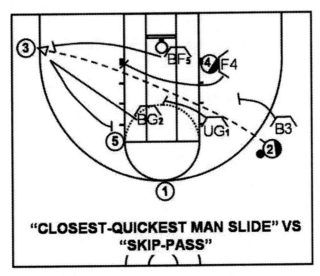

"CLOSEST-QUICKEST MAN SLIDE" VS "SKIP-PASS"

Diagram 6.20

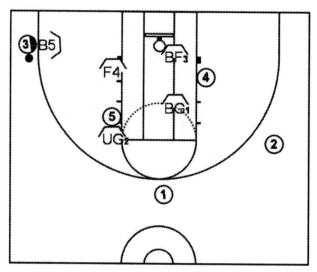

Diagram 6.21

7

Player Box-Out Responsibilities

All of the match-up zone defenses have characteristics of zone defenses, man-to-man defenses, and also varying degrees of half-court trapping defenses (via different stunts). Ideally, the match-up zone incorporates the strengths of each of these three distinctly different types of defenses.

Realistically, the match-up zone also inherits a few of the weaknesses of each defense. Many coaches feel the one commonly known weakness of all zone defenses is the fact that an offensive opponent has the rebounding advantage when their zone offense is playing against your zone defense. This advantage can also exist when an opponent attacks the match-up zone unless the defensive coaching staff first has a strong belief in the importance of defensive boxing out. The coaching staff must then stress that importance to his players by teaching the proper fundamentals of boxing out and defensive rebounding, and then teaching every player the individual responsibilities/assignments for all five defensive positions. These techniques and assignments must be practiced and drilled daily for every player to remember his assignment and also to perfect the actual defensive box-out techniques. These assignments and the correct techniques must not only be stressed, but the coaching staff must demand that they be performed every time the match-up zone forces the opponent to take a shot.

The primary goal of every defense is to prevent the opposition's offense from scoring. The initial defensive goal is to force the opposition into taking poor shots that do not have great chances of being successful. Effectively running the match-up zone should accomplish this first goal.

The second important goal for every match-up defender is to get every defensive rebound after the offense has been forced to take poor shots. To accomplish that goal, each defender must end up between the basket and the man they are assigned to box out. An important secondary goal is to not only stay between the man and the basket, but also to be in the range of where the missed shots will fall.

Defensive rebounders must prevent offensive opponents from pushing them too far under the basket, where only made shot rebounds fall. Defensive rebounds end the opponents' offensive possession and also begin their own offensive possession.

All defenders must make the defensive box-out on the offensive rebounder in their assigned area, whether it is a shooter or a player off of the ball. Every defender that boxes out an offensive opponent should:

- Make the initial contact with the offensive opponent with the defenders' backside into the front of the offensive rebounder. The short phrase used to emphasize that proper concept is for the box-out to "go butt to gut."
- Keep the elbows high and locked with the head up and hands up.
- Use short, choppy steps to maintain contact with the opponent.
- Be sure to not get pushed too far under the basket. If a defender does get physically out-manned and pushed, he should stagger the feet to keep from getting shoved too far under the basket.

Defensive boxing out must be consistently (and constantly) drilled. The correct techniques must first be taught and explained. Then, demand that every defensive player perform them properly all of the time. It must be stressed that no good defense exists to defend against opponents' second shots.

Approaching the opponent before actually making the box-out will vary because defenders have different box-out assignments. These different assignments then will require different methods for the defensive box-out to be successful.

The first technique that must be taught to every match-up defender is that the defender should approach and initiate the contact on the offensive rebounding opponent, and locate himself between the opponent and the basket. To eliminate the guessing of which direction the potential offensive rebounder might go to rebound, coaches should emphasize that these particular defenders must fan the opponent towards the sideline and baseline before then making a reverse pivot off of the foot (closest to the sideline or baseline) to make the contact on the opponent.

Doing so also makes the defenders the actors and forces the offensive players to become the reactors, which forces the offensive players to move in the direction that the defense wants them to go. Fanning the opponents towards the out-of-bounds lines and then remaining between the ball and the opponent puts the defender in ideal position to obtain the majority of rebounds, while minimizing the opposition's chances for gaining repossession of the ball. Once contact is made, all defenders must then maintain that contact with his box-out. Those defenders want to try to initiate that contact outside of the free-throw lane to prevent being pushed under the basket. Three basic methods are generally employed for a match-up defender to successfully perform this necessary responsibility.

Box-out Techniques

Box-out Technique #1

A defender that is guarding the ball—and therefore the shooter—should be closely guarding the shooter from the onset to prevent uncontested and easy shot attempts. He should not have a problem making physical contact with the man he is to box out.

Coaches should use a few short phrases to describe the overall technique of defending the shooter. First, coaches should tell the defender, "Don't foul a jump-shooter." Shooting percentages of contested field-goal attempts are drastically lower than free-throw shot percentages. Coaches should then tell defenders, "Don't leave the ground until the shooter leaves the ground." This prevents defenders from fouling or getting shot-faked and then driven on.

If the shooter is right-handed, coaches should tell the defender to have his left hand up. Doing so places the defensive pressure on the appropriate hand of the shooter. If the shooter is left-handed, the defender should have his right hand up.

When the shot is taken, insist that the defender make a front pivot in the direction that the shooter goes to offensive rebound and then to utilize the four techniques of the actual defensive box-out. If the offensive player steps to his right, have the defender make a front crossover step with his right foot directly into the offensive rebounder to initiate the contact. From there, he uses the three remaining techniques of the actual defensive box-out previously discussed:

- Keep the elbows high and locked and the head and hands up.
- Use choppy steps to maintain physical contact with the opposition's rebounder.

- Stay on the area outside of the rim (see Diagram 7.1). If the offensive player steps to his left, have the defender make a front crossover step with his left foot directly into the offensive rebounder to make the contact (see Diagram 7.2).

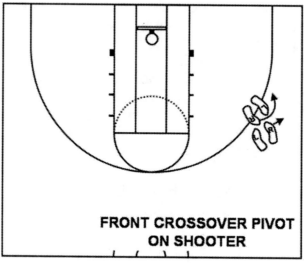

Diagram 7.1

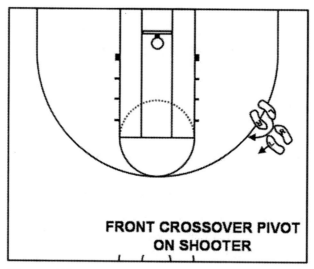

Diagram 7.2

Box-out Technique #2

Oftentimes, the defensive up guard, or possibly the back guard, that is semi-fronting a high-post player has a different and much more difficult box-out technique. He already should be making contact with his opponent, but by semi-fronting him, he is very much out of position and must hustle to get between the offensive rebounder and the basket. His technique will be different than the ball man's technique, because he must react and quickly move to establish the position between the offensive man and the basket. He must actually react like an offensive rebounder who is getting boxed out to get around his opponent. He can accomplish this technique by spinning and using the swim technique and always going around the side that he has shaded in the fronting action. Once he gets around, he can start using the three other actual box-out techniques (see Diagrams 7.3 and 7.4).

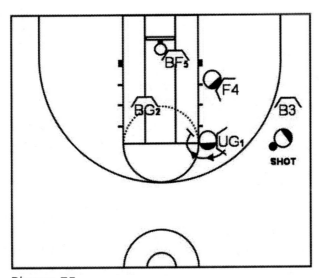

Diagram 7.3

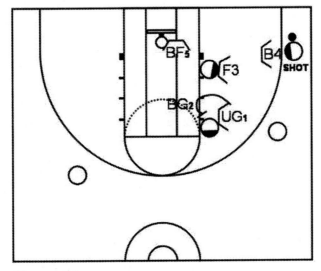

Diagram 7.4

Box-out Technique #3

All other off-the-ball defenders most likely will be the front man, the back forward, the back guard, and sometimes the up guard. These defenders are often in situations where they must box out a defender that is not a shooter or an offensive post player.

The technique of approaching the offensive opponent under control by fanning (cutting to the sideline or baseline) the offensive players allows the defense to take control of the situation. Now that the defenders have a much better idea of which direction the offensive opponents are going, they have a much improved chance initiating contact and therefore being successful in the defensive boxout.

These off-the-ball defenders must first approach the opponent under control and encourage that offensive player to go toward the outside (toward the sideline or baseline) before making a reverse pivot into the offensive player to make physical contact as far from the basket as they possibly can. Doing so prevents the opposition from shoving them further inside underneath the basket where no defensive rebounds live.

Diagrams 7.5 and 7.6 show examples of these box-outs by several defenders on both sides of the floor. Diagram 7.5 shows the back forward (BF5) overplaying 05 by fanning the opposition towards the baseline before then reverse pivoting into the gut of the opponent. The same diagram shows the back guard (BG2) angling down and still fanning the offensive ballside post player (04) toward the baseline. The front man (F4) hustles out under control just one full step towards the perimeter opponent in the deep ballside corner (03) by fanning him toward the baseline. He, too, then reverse pivots and makes the initial contact on the opposition as far from the free throw lane as possible.

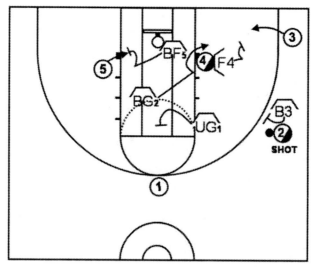

Diagram 7.5

Diagram 7.6 shows the back forward (BF5) closing out on the opponent in the weakside corner area (05) by fanning him before making the reverse pivot. The front man (F3) closes out on the ballside high post (04) and overplays him to fan him before making a reverse pivot into him. The back guard (BG2) fans the weakside high-post player (03) and then reverse pivots into the path the opponent most likely would take to go after the rebound. The up guard makes a quick reverse pivot on the side of the high post (04) that he initially shades (which is the low side since the ball is in the low corner).

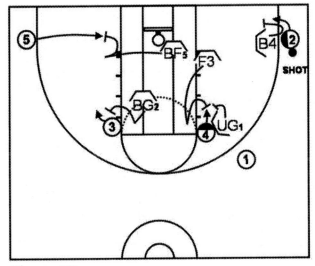

Diagram 7.6

Box-out Responsibilities by Position

Offensive opponents have a multitude of offensive positions that they can occupy before and when the ball is shot. Defenders in each individual position have a specific priority level of whom to box out. Every player must learn the priority levels of each position and box out opponents that are in that priority scheme.

Ball Man

The ball man always boxes out the shooter that he is defending. He has the simplest priority list of all defenders. The ball man is also the only defender that should use the front pivot to initiate the contact with the offensive player. Once contact is made, it is maintained in the same manner that every other defender uses, utilizing the three remaining box-out techniques previously listed.

Front Man

The front man boxes out offensive players as follows: He first makes contact with the ballside low-post player and looks to see if an offensive player is located in the ballside corner (short or deep). The front man's (F4) number one priority is the player located in the open ballside corner. He should not go out after that potential offensive rebounder, but only take one full step toward him (see Diagram 7.7). If no player is in the corner, the front man (F4) should then look for any player located in the ballside high-post area (both an empty and a low call should have been made) (see Diagram 7.8). If no one is in the corner, and no one is in the ballside high post, the front man (F4) should look for his third priority—the ballside low-post area—and then go for that offensive player (see Diagram 7.9). If no player is in any of the three areas, or if he is undecided on whom to box out, the front man should go to the center of the lane at the dotted circle and pick up any opponent that passes through that area (see Diagram 7.10). Notice that the front man always fans the opposition's rebounder towards the baseline.

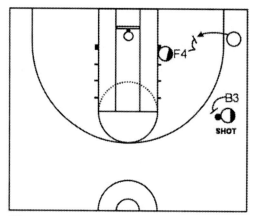

Diagram 7.7

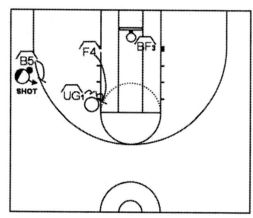

Diagram 7.8

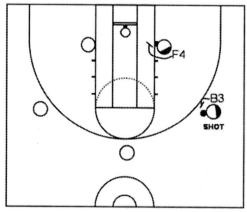

Diagram 7.9

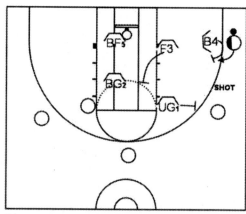

Diagram 7.10

Back Forward

The back forward (BF5) has the most crucial area in the entire match-up zone defense. This area is the most important because the majority of missed shots by opponents' offenses will most likely fall in this particular area on the weakside.

The back forward also will overplay the opposition by forcing him to go toward the baseline. This overplay gives the defenders a more predictable path for the offensive opponent, so that he may successfully box the offensive player out. Forcing the opposition along the baseline also puts the offensive player in a location that is not conducive to offensive rebounding: behind the basket. Thus, the defense has a better chance for successful defensive rebounding. The back forward boxes out offensive players in this particular order:

- The weakside low post (see Diagram 7.11)
- The weakside high post (see Diagram 7.12)
- The weakside wing area (see Diagram 7.13)
- The dotted circle in the middle of the free-throw lane (see Diagram 7.14)

He first looks in the area that is in the number one priority: the weakside low-post area. If an opponent is found in that area, the back forward overplays the rebounder located on the weakside low-post area by fanning him towards the baseline before he makes the reverse pivot. He wants to try to make contact with the offensive rebounder outside of the lane (see Diagram 7.11).

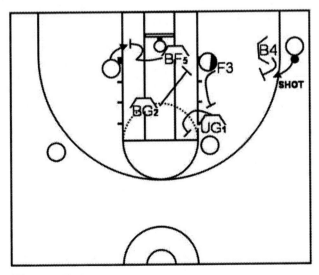

Diagram 7.11

In the next offensive scenario, the back forward (BF5) has no one to box out in the weakside low-post area, so he goes to his second priority: the weakside high-post area. He also fans the offensive high-post player and then boxes him out as far from the basket as he possibly can (see Diagram 7.12).

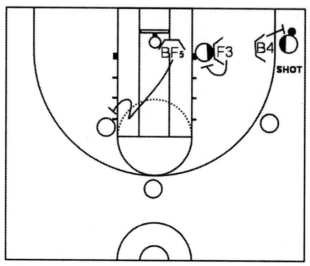

Diagram 7.12

The back forward's third priority is anyone located in the weakside wing area. The back forward (BF5) closes out on that perimeter opponent by making his approach by shading toward the inside shoulder of the opponent. He then makes contact by utilizing a reverse pivot as far from the basket as he possibly can (see Diagram 7.13).

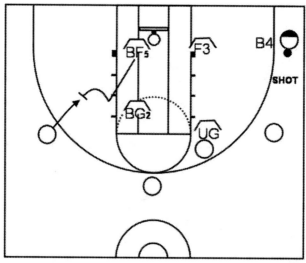

Diagram 7.13

If no offensive opponents are in any of those three areas, his last priority is to head for the dotted circle in the middle of the free-throw lane to pick up any offensive player that crosses his face (see Diagram 7.14).

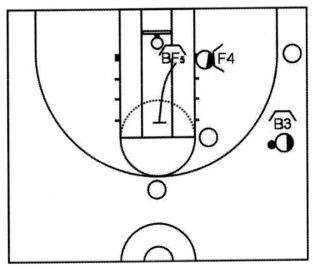

Diagram 7.14

Back Guard

The back guard (BG2) has the second most crucial area in the entire match-up zone defense. The reason is that the offense's (most likely) biggest rebounder is located in his number one priority location:-the ballside low post area. The defense will likely not have a tall back guard compared to the opposition's offensive low-post player. Utilizing the proper techniques in defensive boxing out is probably more important for the defense's back guard than in any other defensive position in the defense.

Getting position advantage and then maintaining that advantage is of tremendous importance to the back guard. The back guard also should overplay the opposition by forcing him to go toward the baseline. This same fanning overplay results in giving defenders the same predictable path for the offensive opponent, so that he may successfully box him out. Forcing the opposition along the baseline also puts offensive players behind the basket, which again is a location that is not conducive to offensive rebounding. The back guard boxes out offensive players in this particular priority order:

- First, the ballside low post (see Diagram 7.15).
- Then, the weakside high post (see Diagram 7.16).
- And finally, the dotted circle in the middle of the free-throw lane (see Diagram 7.17).

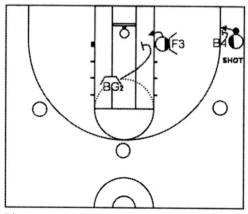

Diagram 7.15

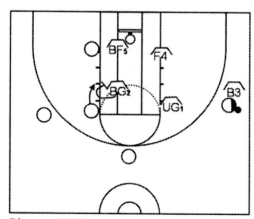

Diagram 7.16

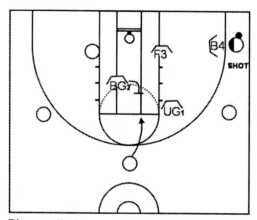

Diagram 7.17

Up Guard

The up guard also will overplay the opposition by forcing him to go toward the sideline, for the same reasons that all other defenders fan their respective assignments. Doing so gives the defense a better chance for successful defensive rebounding. The up guard boxes out offensive players in this particular priority order.

- First, the up guard should box out the open ballside wing (see Diagram 7.18).
- Next, the up guard should box out the ballside high post (see Diagram 7.19).
- Then, the up guard should look for any "wrong-colored jersey" passing through anywhere near the dotted circle in the middle of the free-throw lane (see Diagram 7.20).

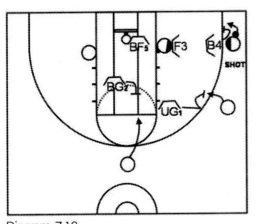

Diagram 7.18

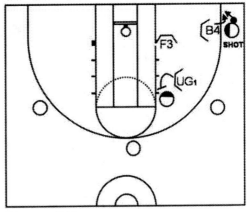

Diagram 7.19

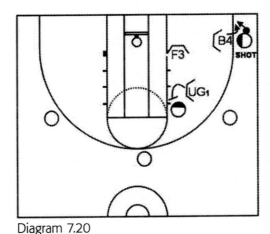

Diagram 7.20

Box-Out Responsibilities of All Defenders in the Match-Up Zone Defense

Front Man
1. Low post and anyone coming from the ballside corner
2. Low post and anyone coming from the ballside high post
3. Ballside low post
4. Dotted circle in the middle of the free-throw lane

Back Forward
1. Weakside low post
2. Weakside high post
3. Weakside wing
4. Dotted circle in the middle of the free-throw lane

Up Guard
1. Open ballside wing
2. Ballside high post
3. Dotted circle in the middle of the free-throw lane

Back Guard
1. Ballside low post
2. Weakside high post
3. Dotted circle in the middle of the free-throw lane

Ball Man
1. The shooter

Figure 7.1

8

Stunts

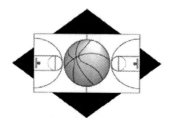

Stunts from the multiple match-up zone defense and the different initial defensive alignments are what make the match-up zone a multiple type of defense. The defensive stunts are very difficult for an opponent to scout and therefore to prepare for. More importantly, it gives a defensive team the mindset that they are the team that is in control—not the offense. The defensive team becomes the actors and the opposition's offensive team must then become the reactors and attempt to counteract whatever defensive stunt is used to attack them.

Any one of these stunts could possibly uncover offensive deficiencies that can then continually be attacked and taken advantage of until the opposition can correct it. When a defensive team has stunts that it can utilize at any point in time, it makes it extremely difficult for an offensive team to be able to find that important offensive rhythm that is often needed to be successful. This chapter lists the stunts that can easily be added to the defensive repertoire to make the defense the aggressor. They are not a requirement of the match-up zone, but are valuable additions that can be extremely important to the overall defensive scheme.

You want to consider two things in making your defensive game plans. You would not want to (nor should you) teach all the stunts in any one year if your personnel could not handle it, and you would want to choose the stunts that would give your next opponent the most problems. These seventeen different stunts are:

- Hard
- Jump
- Double
- Hard-Double
- Jump-Double
- Smash
- Double-Smash
- Read
- Double-Read

- Choke
- Double-Choke
- Lock
- Left-Lock
- Right-Lock
- Bullet
- Left-Bullet
- Right-Bullet

An imaginative coach could probably come up with additional stunts to add or substitute with these stunts. In many cases, almost every stunt has been incorporated during the same year, but every stunt does not have to be utilized during the same season and most definitely does not have to be used in every game.

If the defensive team can handle the mental challenge, the old adage "the more, the better" could be very appropriate. Even if the defense utilizes many match-up stunts and opposing offenses perceive the defense to be more complicated, the defense remains simple with the base defense concept. This concrete concept should be implemented by the defensive team to teach them that after every stunt has been performed, the defense then reverts back to the base defense of the match-up defense. Doing so keeps the defense in a method of attack that is simplified for all defenders and yet this defense is an aggressive, attacking, and searching-for-offensive-weaknesses type of defense that opposing offenses must attempt to figure out and counter.

Hard Stunt

The hard stunt is valuable because it can be so simple and yet so potentially disruptive for the opposition. In the hard stunt, the defensive up guard extends himself and places as much one-on-one defensive pressure as he can physically place on the ballhandler. The defensive pick-up point could be as much as full-court defensive pressure to as little as the front court's sideline hash marks. This simple stunt actually is performed only by the up guard while all the remaining defenders align themselves and utilize the same techniques as they normally do.

This stunt makes it appear that the defense is now in a man-to-man defense and not a match-up zone or any form of a zone defense at all. Many opponents then adjust and change their offense, which sometimes leads them to operate out of an offense that can be inadequate against the standard match-up zone defense.

The hard stunt can definitely destroy the rhythm and the confidence of the opposition's offense. The hard stunt will challenge the opposition's point guard and give the defensive team and its coaching staff a very safe way to investigate and analyze the opposition's ballhandling and passing skills. If it is determined that those skills are not a weakness, that evaluation can be made without the defense paying a price.

Determining that the offense has a hidden weakness that has been uncovered by running hard, many other complimentary stunts can then be attempted to attack that newfound deficiency in the opposition's offense. If a point guard weakness is discovered, it is capitalized upon until the weakness is repaired or corrected. An additional advantage can be that the original up guard can easily and effectively influence the side of the floor on which he wants the offense to start, instead of the offense making that choice (see Diagram 8.1).

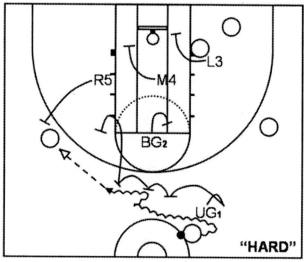

Diagram 8.1

Still another advantage of the hard stunt is the simplicity of it, because it actually involves only the defense's up guard; after the first pass is made, the stunt is over and the defense is back to its normal mode—the base defense. A coaching point that should be emphasized to each and every player is that once the offensive point guard (01) successfully makes the wing pass, the hard stunt is completely over and the defense is back to the base defense (see Diagram 8.2).

Sometimes after the first wing pass, the back guard must become the next up guard (if there is an offensive high post that needs to immediately be covered and the wing pass goes to the side where the high post player is located), while the extended up guard gets back to the normal coverage area of the back guard (see Diagram 8.3).

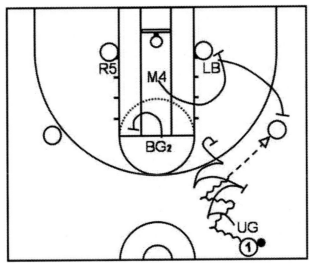

Diagram 8.2

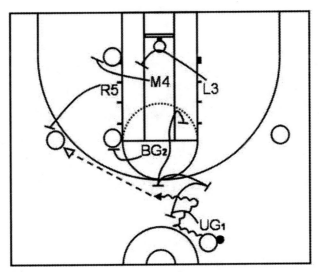

Diagram 8.3

Jump Stunt

Once the defense has executed the hard stunt at the opposition a couple of times, the natural progression is to have the defense follow with another pressure defensive stunt. This progression stunt that should follow the hard stunt is called jump.

When an offense has received a steady dose of the hard stunt, the offense will eventually learn to effectively handle the stunt by doing specific things to counter and defeat the hard stunt. But if they would continue to attack the defense in the same manner against the defense's jump stunt, the offense would play right into the defense's hands. The offense will have a very difficult time in determining which stunt (if any) is going to develop as the ball is being brought down the court.

The main techniques of the jump stunt that must be taught and emphasized are that the original up guard must pressure and turn the ballhandler back into the middle of the floor in the front court. The back guard must read the dribbler and anticipate when his teammate is going to force the dribbler back into the middle of the floor so he can attack the dribbler from the blind side, which is where the jump will take place.

If the offensive point guard can handle the pressure and he effectively passes the ball out of the surprise jump-stunt trap, the jump stunt is completely over and the base match-up zone continues without any hesitation. The standard match-up zone is back in place, with the original up guard following the pass out of the trap and going to the ballside high-post area, while remaining as the up guard. The (jumping) back guard rotates back and remains as the back guard.

If the backline players (L3 and R4) can anticipate where the pass will be thrown out of the trap and still defend the area closest to the basket, they can sometimes take calculated actions and look for an interception. If not successful, they must then recover and become the standard ball man in the match-up zone. The opportunity that the stunt gives the defense does not cost the defense anything now that it is back in place (see Diagram 8.4).

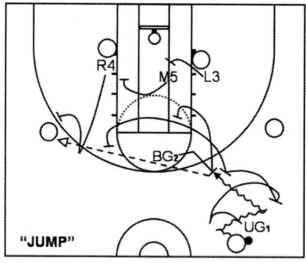

Diagram 8.4

Double Stunt

Still another ball-pressure stunt that attacks and probes potential weaknesses of perimeter players other than the point guard is called the double stunt. The double stunt should be run only after the first pass is made to the wing. The typical wing slide is made by the new ball man after the wing pass is made by the offensive point guard (01) to the perimeter player on the wing (02). But the up guard (UG1) follows the pass and double-teams the ball with the new ball man (L3), attacking the new ballhandler (02) (see Diagram 8.5).

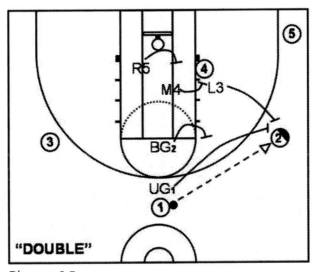

Diagram 8.5

In addition to attacking the ballhandler, this stunt can be utilized to minimize the offensive capabilities of specific opponents and also to discourage that offense from actually passing the ball to that player. The double stunt simply puts double-team pressure on the ball only after the offensive point guard has surrendered the ball and passed the first pass to the wing area. If the wing player can handle the surprising and double-team pressure and effectively passes the ball out of the double-team trap, the double stunt is completely over and the base match-up zone is back in effect. If the ball is down-passed to the deep corner, the normal down slide is executed again. If the ball is reverse passed to the top of the key, the initial back guard (BG2) must become the new up guard while the initial (trapping) up guard (UG1) must rotate back to become the new back guard (see Diagram 8.6).

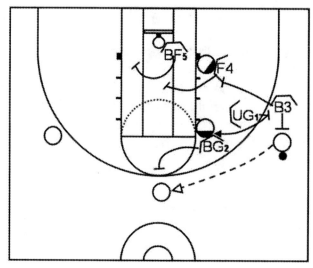

Diagram 8.6

Hard-Double and Jump-Double Stunts

These two stunts can actually be run in unison with hard or with jump. This possible combination of hard-double or jump-double gives an entirely different appearance of the match-up zone. Different appearances of defenses cause opposing offenses to take the time to observe, evaluate, and eventually make decisions on how to proceed. Those evaluations (and the resulting decisions on the plan of attack) can very easily be incorrect, which usually results in advantages and positive results for the defense (see Diagram 8.7 for an example of the jump-double stunt).

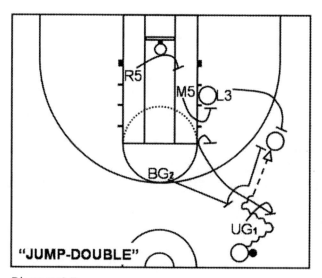

Diagram 8.7

Smash Stunt

The smash stunt is predicated upon any pass that is defined as a down pass. If a down pass is never made, then the pre-called smash stunt can never be executed. But if a down pass is made and the smash stunt has been called, this defensive stunt is in effect until the ball has escaped the first trap in the deep corner. It must be emphasized again that after any stunt is executed, the stunt is completely over and the defense is back to the base defense. In Diagram 8.8, the ball is on the defense's left wing area, with the initial ball man being B3 and the initial front man being F4. The smash stunt is a defensive stunt that involves the initial ball man (B3) and the initial front man (F4). With the ball being down-passed to a pass receiver (O5) in the deep-corner area, the initial front man (F4) closes out on the pass receiver the same way he does while in the base defense. The difference is that the initial ball man (B3) does not run a down slide to become the new front man, but instead takes an inside-out angle and then attacks the ball (with the original front man). The initial back forward (BF5) executes his normal technique of quickly three-quarter fronting the offensive low post on the low side of him. But instead of getting bumped off by the initial ball man (B3), he stays to defend the low post. The two trappers (B3 and F4) should L-trap with their feet and cross-face with their extended arms. The initial up guard (UG1) then steps out so that he is between the ballside elbow area and the offensive wing at the free-throw line extended. The up guard's (UG1) normal pistols stance should be changed to the intercept stance, so that he is facing the offensive ballhandler and the trap in the deep corner. He should read the passer's eyes and react to the escape pass, particularly to the ballside wing or to the high post.

The back guard (BG2) should be in the normal pistols stance and location and anticipate a possible skip pass to the top of the key or to the weakside wing area. Again, it is extremely important for all five defenders to realize that once the ball has escaped the trap, the smash stunt is completely over and the normal base defense is back in effect (see Diagram 8.8).

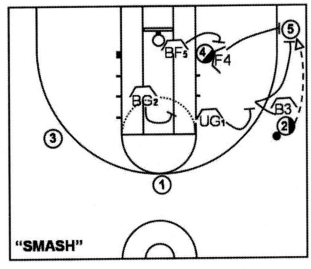

Diagram 8.8

Double Smash

A combination of the double stunt and the smash stunt can be easily utilized to create a new stunt that effectively disguises the match-up and makes it appear to be a fully committed half-court trap defense. Again, once the first smash stunt has been executed, the stunt is completely over. Diagram 8.9 will demonstrate the first wing pass being made to the defense's right side. On the first wing pass (from O1 to O3), the double stunt is executed with the initial ball man (B5) and the up guard (UG1) (see Diagram 8.9).

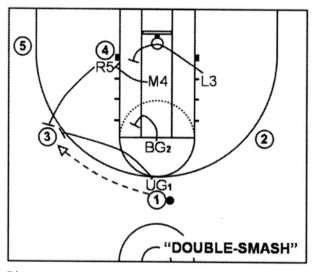

Diagram 8.9

If the ball is then reversed (from O3 to O1), the complete stunt is over and the initial back guard (BG2) and the initial up guard (UG1) switch assignments and continue the base defense of the match-up zone defense (see Diagram 8.10). This reversal pass cancels out the double smash stunt.

But if the ball is down-passed out of the first double action (from O3 to O5), the second part of the original combination stunt is in effect. The first ball man (B5) makes the inside-out cut to close down on the ball in the deep corner. The first front man (F4) closes out on the ball and both players again use the no lines-no splits technique and then trap the ball. The new back forward (BF3) three-quarter fronts the low post from the baseline side, the first up guard (UG1) opens up to the ball and splits the difference between the ballside wing and the ballside high post in his intercept stance, and the first back guard (BG2) remains in the pistols stance and anticipates a possible escape skip pass out of the hard trap (see Diagram 8.11).

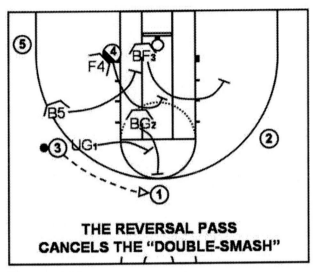

Diagram 8.10

Diagram 8.11

Read Stunt

The read stunt is another stunt that can only be utilized only after the opposition's offense makes a down pass that follows a wing pass. If a wing pass is made, but is followed by a reversal pass (02 to 01), this particular stunt cannot yet be run. On the reversal pass, everyone is centered up and the base defense of the match-up zone is back in effect.

But when a down pass is made (from 02 to 04 after the wing pass), the other four defenders jump to the ball and execute the normal down slide. In this illustration of the down slide, the first front man (F4) closes out on the ball in the deep corner, the original ball man (B3) reacts quickly and becomes the new front man, the initial back forward (BF5) comes around on the baseline side and three-quarter fronts the low post on the ballside, and the back guard (BG2) plays the down pass in the same manner as usual.

The original up guard (UG1) opens up to the ball in his intercept stance and faces the ballhandler in the deep corner. He anticipates an up pass, a pass to the high post, or a skip pass to the top of the key. The proper techniques, stances, and location/positioning (especially by the up guard) will determine the success of this particular match-up zone stunt (see Diagram 8.12).

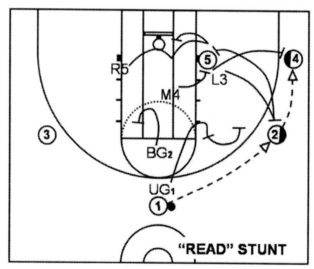

Diagram 8.12

Double Read Stunt

Another combination stunt that could be utilized is putting together the double stunt (on the first wing pass) and then utilizing the read stunt if the offense makes a down pass to the corner area. Again, if the wing pass is made (from 01 to 03), the double stunt is executed. But if the offense chooses to escape pass out of the double-team trap in the wing area to the top of the key (03 to 01), the second half of this stunt is voided by that reversal pass. The usual centered up slide is executed instead and all five defenders are back in the base defense of the match-up.

Diagram 8.13 shows the offense making a pass to the defense's right wing area. The up guard (UG1) executes the initial part of the stunt with the new ball man (B5). With no ball reversal pass made and instead a down pass is made, the final half of the stunt can be executed. The initial ball man (B5) makes his usual down slide to cover the low post, while the back forward (BF3) helps to cover the low post for an instant. The first front man (F4) closes out on the ball (O5) to become the new ball man The up guard leaves the double-team trap and, with an open pistols stance, stays in an area between the ballside wing area and the ballside high post area. He is reading the passer's eyes to determine where the up pass is going (see Diagrams 8.14 and 8.15).

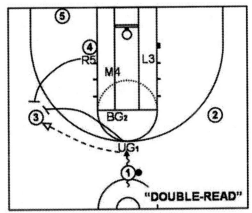

Diagram 8.13

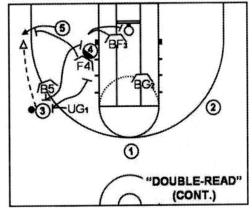

Diagram 8.14

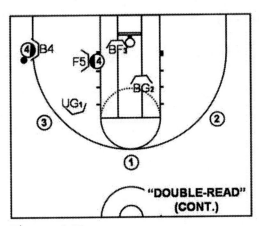

Diagram 8.15

Choke Stunt

A stunt somewhat complimentary to the read stunt, called the choke stunt, can be executed to either side of the floor, but only after a down pass is made. After the first down pass is made by the opposition's offense, the stunt is executed and finished.

In order to run the choke stunt, the opposition's offense must first make a wing pass that is followed by a down pass to a player in the corner. On the wing pass that is followed by the defense's wing slide, every defender appears to be in the base defense of the match-up.

If the offense then makes the down pass, it appears that the defense makes a down slide and that the usual match-up defense is in effect. The initial ball man (B3) rotates to cover the ballside low-post player as the new front man. The initial front man (F4) closes out on the ballhandler in the deep corner (O5) and becomes the new ball man. If there is an offensive post player on the ballside (O4), a low call should be made. The initial back forward (BF5) comes around on the baseline side to three-quarter front him until the new front man (F3) gets there on his particular down slide action (from the original down passer).

But in reality, the stunt has just begun. Instead of the new up guard staying in tight and protecting the ballside high-post area and allowing the offense to up-pass the ball at will, the choke stunt simply encourages the offense to get the ball down in the corner and then not allow the ball to be passed out of that area. The up guard fully commits to denying the up pass (form O5 to O2).

On the choke stunt, the up guard (UG1) does not split the difference between the high post and the wing (as he does in a read stunt) but overplays defensively and steps out to deny the pass from the deep corner to the wing by defending him as if he were playing him in a man-to-man denial defense.

If a ballside high-post player is utilized (should be a high call), the back guard (BG2) extends himself over to help defend him. If no ballside high-post player is used (should be a open call), the back guard anticipates a skip pass out of the deep corner to the weakside wing area (O3) or the top of the key area (O1). He sits in his pistols stance, points to the ball and the wing area (with his head on a swivel) from his correct location (man-side [MS] line at the dotted circle) and is ready for the interception or deflection of the skip pass.

This stunt can quickly lead to interceptions out of the deep corner or at least disrupt the opposition's offensive rhythm and discourage the pass down to the deep corner (see Diagram 8.16). But if the offense never down-passes the ball and chooses to immediately reverse the ball from the wing area to the top of the key, the choke stunt is immediately over before it actually starts and the defense executes the centered up slide on the reversal pass. The choke stunt is called off and the defense is back to the base defense of the match-up zone defense.

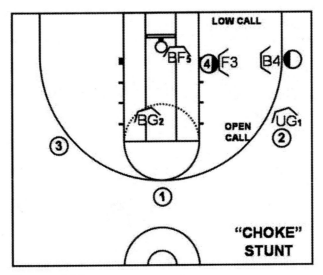

Diagram 8.16

Double-Choke Stunt

Another combination stunt that can be easily incorporated in the defensive stunt scheme of the match-up zone defense package is called the double-choke stunt. This stunt is just a combination of the double stunt followed by the choke stunt. It gives the defense still another look, a different method of attack on the offense, while not sacrificing any of the defense's simplicity of the base defense.

Diagrams 8.17 and 8.18 illustrate the first wing pass being made to the defense's left side. This pass causes the first ball man (B3) and the first up guard (UG1) to double-team the ball at the wing area (02) on the left side of the floor (see Diagram 8.17). Again, if the ball is immediately reversed to the top of the key (from 02 to 01), the overall stunt is then over.

If the defense trapped the first wing pass and the offense escaped out of the trap and reversed the ball, then the defensive team is back to the base defense of the match-up zone with no (second choke) stunt on. But if the ball is successfully down-passed (from 02 to 05), the new ball man (B4) is on the ball, the new front man (F3) is in the correct position and stance to deny the inside pass, while the same back forward (BF5) and back guard (BG2) remain in the backline to support the pressure part of the defense. The up guard (UG1) steps out in a defensive overplay position and stance to completely deny the up pass (from 05 to 02) out of the corner. The back guard should remain in the proper position and stance to anticipate an attempted escape pass out of the corner to either the ballside high-post area, the weakside wing area, or the top of the key. Those three positions are not impossible for the back guard to defend (if he remains in the proper stance and location). If the ball man executes the proper techniques of pressuring the basketball to force a high lob pass out of the corner, that lob pass must travel a long distance in the air. This extra time would then give the back guard plenty of time to react and go for the interception, or at least a deflection.

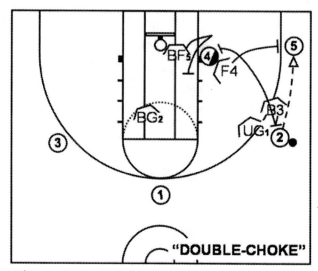

Diagram 8.17

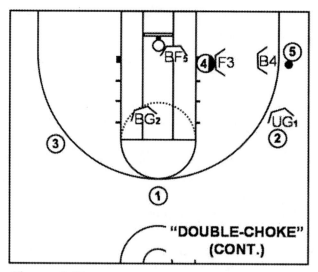

Diagram 8.18

Lock and Bullet Stunts

Two of the most effective stunts that can be utilized are the lock and bullet stunts. They are unique from the other stunts in that, from the perspective of the offense, the entire defensive scheme of the match-up zone changes instantly and seemingly without warning. These two stunts also stand out as different from the others because once these stunts are into play, they remain in place. The lock and bullet stunts are very similar to each other and differ only from their trigger points—when the offensive action triggers the defense into the actual start of the called stunt. Both stunts could be run for only one pre-designated side of the floor or for either side of the floor. The number of stunts thus expands to an accumulated total of six different stunts—left lock, right lock, left bullet, right bullet, lock, or bullet.

The first stunt described is the lock stunt. Its so-called "trigger point" is when a pre-designated wing pass is made. The stunt could be expanded to become only a left lock or a right lock or lock to either side. For instance, if a left lock is called, that would trigger the defense to activate that stunt every time the wing pass is made only to the defensive left side of the court.

In the usual wing slide of the match-up zone defense, the original left man (L3) would close out on the ball to become the match-up's ball man. The original middle man (M4) would normally come around to front the low post and be the first front man. The original right man (R5) would provide helpside support by becoming the back forward, while the two guards would become the up guard and the back guard. But in this case, if the offensive action triggered the defensive stunt, the ball man would close out on the ball as usual.

But at that point, everything would change. The defender (L3) who closed out on the ball would take the ball but would lock onto him in a man-to-man defensive scheme. All the off-the-ball defenders would instantly search for the closest man (that they should logically match up with) and also lock onto that player in a man-to-man type of action. The middle man would have to take the ballside low-post player.

Diagrams 8.19 and 8.20 illustrate different offensive scenarios that would show how defenders would properly match up with and lock onto the appropriate offensive players. Every player would stay with his man-to-man responsibility until a change in possession of the basketball. Man-to-man defensive concepts and philosophies—such as fanning the ball and three-quarter fronting the ballside low post, jumping to the ball, pistols stances, ball-you-man flat triangle positioning, and so forth—come into play immediately when the lock stunt is initiated. The only exception would be if two defenders could safely switch men because of match-up problems during an offensive lull in the action.

If a right lock stunt is called and the ball is passed to the defense's left side of the floor, the stunt is immediately voided and called off. The base defense of the match-up zone is immediately in effect. If a lock stunt is called, that means that the stunt is initiated on the wing pass, regardless of what side of the floor the pass is made. Diagram 8.19 shows X5 closing out on 03 on the ball, X1 on 01, X2 on 02, X3 on 04, and X4 on 05. Diagram 8.20 shows X3 on 02, X1 on 01, X2 on 03, X4 on 05, and X5 on 04 (at the high post). Even though X2 is closer to 04 and X5 is closer to 03, X2 should lock onto 03 and X5 should lock on to 04, because of the more suitable defensive match-ups.

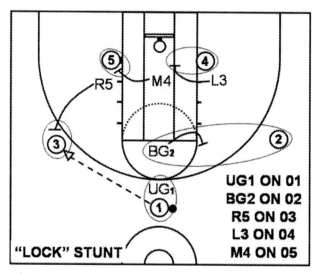

UG1 ON 01
BG2 ON 02
R5 ON 03
L3 ON 04
M4 ON 05

"LOCK" STUNT

Diagram 8.19

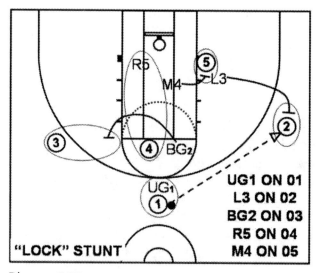

UG1 ON 01
L3 ON 02
BG2 ON 03
R5 ON 04
M4 ON 05

"LOCK" STUNT

Diagram 8.20

Diagram 8.21 illustrates how the match-up zone defenders literally match up to offensive players in the lock stunt after the wing pass is made: UG1 on 01, L3 on 02, BG2 on 03, M4 on 04, and R5 on 05.

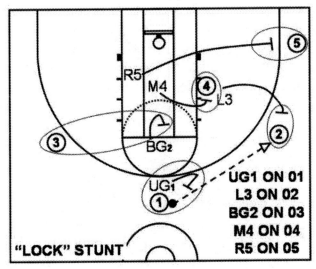

Diagram 8.21

Diagram 8.22 illustrates the same offensive alignment, but with the initial wing pass going to the opposite side of the floor. This switch causes defensive responsibilities to become: UG1 on 01, BG2 on 02, R5 on 03, M4 on 04, and L3 on 05. If the defensive assignments of R5 on 03 and L3 on 05 present a mismatch, they could utilize a defensive switch only during an opportune time for the defense.

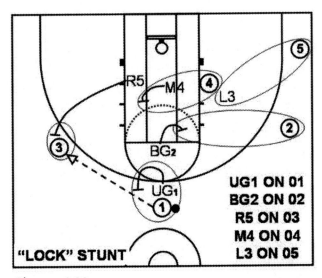

Diagram 8.22

The bullet stunt is a stunt that can be run on either side of the defensive floor (bullet) or on just a specifically designated side of the court (left bullet or right bullet). Any of these three stunts are initiated only on the first down pass to the deep corner, which means that a wing pass must first take place. This wing pass initiates the match-up zone's standard wing slide, with a ball man (B3) from the backline of the zone closing out on the ball (O2); a front man (F4) fronting any ballside low-post players (O4) in a complete fronting stance; and the back forward (BF5), the up guard (UG1), and the back guard (BG2) aligning in their normal, proper stances and positions/locations to give the opposition the appearance of the regular match-up zone defense (see Diagram 8.23).

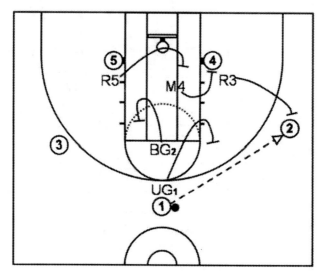

Diagram 8.23

When the down pass is made to a side that is not appropriate for the specific bullet stunt to be run, the defense remains as the base defense of the match-up zone, with the initial front man (F4) closing out on the ball (O5) and becoming the new ball man. The initial ball man (B3) rotates down and becomes the new front man, while the initial back forward (BF5) comes around to momentarily cover the low post. The up guard (UG1) and the back guard (BG2) stay in the proper positions/locations and the correct stances as they would in the regular match-up zone, because the defense is the usual match-up zone defense (see Diagram 8.24).

Whenever the ball is on the active side for any of the bullet stunts and the ball is immediately reversed to the top of the key after the initial wing pass is made, the stunt is also negated and all five defenders are back to the base defense in the match-up zone after the centered up slide is executed (see Diagram 8.25).

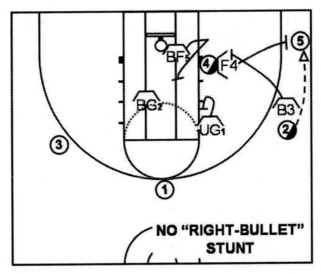

Diagram 8.24

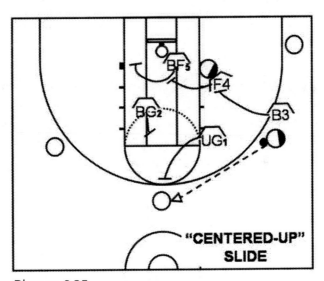

Diagram 8.25

Diagram 8.26 shows the defensive rotations and match-ups when the wing slide is executed immediately after the wing pass is made. The down pass is made on the appropriate side for the stunt to be executed (whether it is the regular bullet stunt or the left bullet stunt). In this particular offensive set, all five defenders rotate and pick up their new man-to-man responsibilities. The original front man (F4) closes out on the ball and takes 05, while the original back forward (BF5) rotates over to pick up the ballside low-post player (04). The original ball man (B3) stays on the original passer

(02), while the up guard (UG1) takes the man closest to him (01) and the original back guard (BG2) finds the closest man (03).

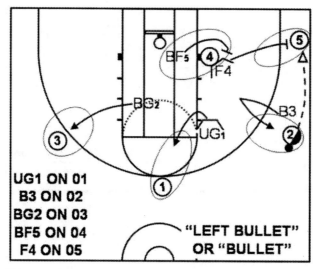

Diagram 8.26

Diagram 8.27 shows the wing pass that is made in a different offensive alignment. The initial ball man (B3) closes out on the ball (02), while the first front man (F4) fronts the offensive low-post player on the ballside (05). The back forward (BF5), the back guard (BG2), and the up guard (UG1) all rotate into the proper positions and the correct stances of the base defense.

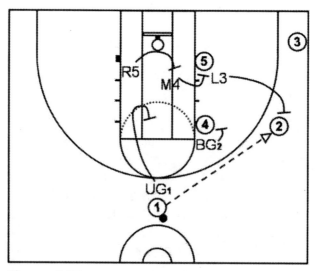

Diagram 8.27

By all appearances of all five defenders, the defense is in the usual base defense of the match-up zone. When the down pass is made to the appropriate deep corner (02 to 03), all five defenders rotate to their opposing player responsibilities. Diagram 8.28 illustrates where the original ball man (B3) rotates to take the ballside high post, the up guard (UG1) steps out to take 02 on the wing, the original front man (F4) closes out on the ball on 03, the back forward comes around to three-quarter front the ballside low post (05), and the back guard (BG2) takes the remaining perimeter player (01). The reason B3 takes 04 instead of 02 and that UG1 takes 02 instead of 04 is to make sure their man-to-man assignments are more compatible.

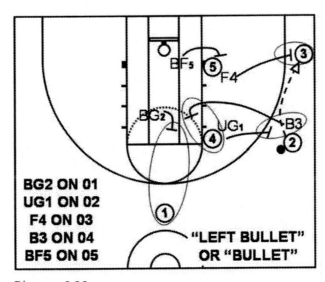

Diagram 8.28

It must be emphasized again that if the left lock or the right lock stunts are called, the ball must be passed to the appropriate wing to activate the specific stunt. If not, the stunt that is called cannot and should not be executed. If the lock stunt is called and as soon as a wing pass is made to either wing, that specific pass activates the lock stunt.

Also it must be stressed that if the left bullet or the right bullet stunts are called, the ball has to be passed to the correct deep corner so that that particular stunt can be run. If those conditions do not take place, the stunt is called off.

The lock stunt is activated when the wing pass is made. The bullet stunt is activated when a wing pass is made and that wing pass is followed by a corner pass. The team stays in their man-to-man defense for the entire possession. Neither stunt can be called off once the stunt begins.

Stunt	Triggered off of what action	Involving what defenders
Hard	Point guard's dribble	Up guard
Jump	Point guard's dribble	Up guard and back guard
Double	Point guard's wing pass	Up guard and ball man
Hard-jump combo	Point guard's dribble	Up guard and back guard
Jump-double combo	Point guard's dribble and wing pass	Up guard, back guard, and ball man
Smash	All down passes	Ball man and front man
Double-smash	After all wing passes and down passes	Up guard, ball man, and front man
Read	All down passes	Up guard
Double-read	All wing passes and down passes	Up guard and ball man
Choke	All down passes	Up guard
Double-choke	All wing passes and down passes	Up guard and ball man
Lock	All wing passes	All five defenders
Left lock	Wing pass only to the left	All five defenders
Right lock	Wing pass only to the right	All five defenders
Bullet	All down passes	All five defenders
Left bullet	Down passes only to the left	All five defenders
Right bullet	Down passes only to the right	All five defenders

Figure 8.1

9

Variations of Defensive Alignments/Sets

Besides the 0 zone in the 1-1-3 alignment, a team can very easily make a cosmetic change in the base defense and move the up guard and the back guard from a vertical tandem to a horizontal tandem. This change makes the defensive alignment a 2-3 zone alignment and should be used when the opposition's offense attempts to attack the 0 zone with a two-guard offensive front. Changing to the 2 zone allows the defense to immediately match up with the offense's zone offense two-guard alignment. All of the slides and the stunts of the 0 zone can easily be implemented in the 2-zone defensive package. The terminology, slides, and stunts remain the same (see Diagram 9.1).

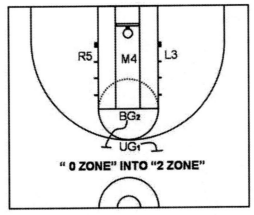

Diagram 9.1

Still another defense that can be added to a team's defensive arsenal of attack could be incorporating the 3 zone. This zone defense is simply walking L3 and R5 of the 0 zone up to the free-throw line extended.

Again, all of the defensive terminology, slides, and stunts of the 0 zone can be executed out of the 3 zone. This substitution gives the defense another cosmetic change in its appearance of the match-up, which in turn gives the opposition more difficulty in predicting and understanding the defense, while not causing the defense any added effort, either physically or mentally (see Diagram 9.2).

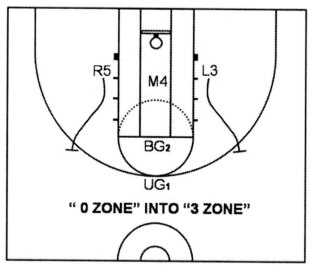

"0 ZONE" INTO "3 ZONE"

Diagram 9.2

Having the variations of the match-up zone defense by utilizing and incorporating the 0 zone, the 2 zone, and the 3 zone will not encumber the defensive team mentally because the defensive terminology, slides, box-out assignments and responsibilities, and stunts are all the same regardless of what defense is being executed.

To the opposition, the 0 zone, the 2 zone, and the 3 zone are perceived to be three unique and separate defensive entities that pose different problems immediately from the cosmetic appearance that each defense possesses. With the changing of the defense, the initial alignment of the defense can actually solve an important problem for the defense when the opposition has counterattacked the defense with a different offensive alignment. Changing the offensive alignment most likely not only changes the appearance of the zone offense, but also changes the zone offense to be executed.

The opposition most likely will have a limited number of zone offenses, each having its own strengths and weaknesses, which can take a mental toll on the opposition's offensive team. But when the defense changes from one of the three possible match-up zone defenses to another, it only appears to become a drastic counter measure and a complete change to another defense. In reality, the defensive change is only a cosmetic change.

The defense can possess three different and unique match-up zone defenses that will not tax the defensive team but can weigh heavily on the opposition. The defensive team gains a sense of being very multiple, complex, difficult to predict, and therefore to solve. But in fact, the defense retains the simplicity once the initial match-up zone defense has been selected, taught, and mastered.

The defensive team should utilize this tremendous advantage over the opposition. Not much extra teaching and practice time should be needed for a defensive team to incorporate at least two, if not all three of these defenses. Yet, the offensive team must expend much more time, energy, and effort in installing and learning additional zone offenses to try to negate the match-up zone defenses.

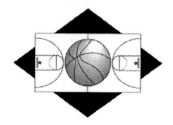

Methods to Defend Specific Offensive Actions

From experience in utilizing the various defensive sets of the match-up zone and seeing how offensive opponents have attempted to attack the match-up zone, what follows is a list of some of the methods opponents have used to attack the defense. These methods are some of the best ways to defend these specific offensive actions.

Versus Short-Corner Offensive Action

The first type of offensive action described is the short-corner action on the ballside. The primary advantage of offensive short-corner action is to raise doubt by the defense on who should cover the player located in the short corner. Three possible coverages could be used. It is more important that whatever coverage is chosen, that method must be thoroughly taught and practiced repeatedly to eliminate the confusion and the slightest doubt of each and every player. The most effective coverage is having the original back forward (BF5) close out on the ball when the short-corner pass is made (see Diagram 10.1). The original ball man (B3) rotates down to become the new front man while the original front man remains on the "block" until B3 gets to him. B3 then pushes F4 across the lane to become the new back forward.

The second method is to always trap (smash stunt) every pass made to the short corner. Doing so has the effect of reducing passes into the short corner. If the opponents know you are going to trap every pass to the short corner, they may not

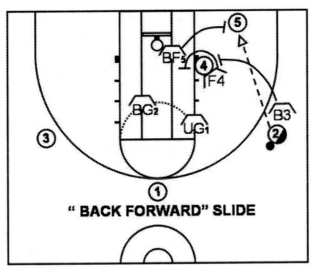

Diagram 10.1

favor passing to the short corner. This trap can be done by executing an automatic smash stunt anytime the short-corner pass is made. This automatic defensive action is executed with the original back forward (BF5) closing out on the baseline while the original ball man (B3) makes the (same) inside-out angle on his approach to the ball in the short-corner area.

As in the typical smash stunt, the ballside low post (04) must be covered. In this case, the low post will be covered by the original front man (F4). When the first wing pass is made, F4 fronts the low post. When the short-corner pass is made to 05 (see Diagram 10.2), the original ball man (B3 in this diagram) traps the ball with the original back forward (BF5) while the original front man (F4) remains on the offensive ballside post player (04).

A third option could be for the defense to choose to automatically execute the choke stunt every time the opposition makes the short-corner pass along the baseline. The choke stunt makes it very difficult to pass the ball out of the short corner. If the offensive player in the short corner who received the pass cannot shoot or drive and has difficulty passing out of the short-corner area, the offense becomes ineffective.

The choke stunt could also serve to discourage the offense from making that pass down to the short-corner area. On the actual pass made to the short-corner, the original back forward (BF5) takes the short-corner pass receiver (05) to become the new ball man, while the original ball man (B3) runs his normal down slide to take over the coverage on the ballside low-post area (04) and become the new front man. The original front man (F4) does not go out on the ball in the corner (as he usually does in the base defense) but stays on the ballside low post (04) until he is pushed out of that specific coverage (by B3) to become the new back forward. The original up guard (UG1) executes the usual choke stunt by stepping out and over to deny the up pass (this time) of any player (02) at the ballside wing from the short-corner player with the ball (see Diagram 10.3).

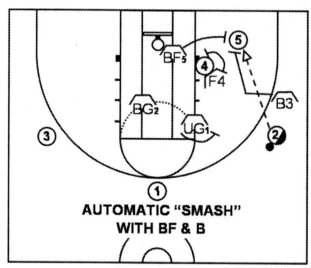

Diagram 10.2

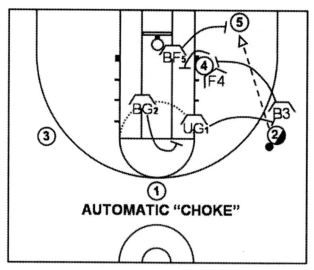

Diagram 10.3

The fourth defensive option is for the defense to automatically execute another stunt that will discourage the offense from running offensive short-corner action. The stunt that could be utilized is the bullet stunt. Again, if the pass is made by the opposition to the pass receiver (05) in the ballside short-corner area, the defense's original back forward (BF5) closes out on the ball. The original front man (F4) remains on the ballside low post (04) and the original ball man (B3) does not make the typical down slide but remains in the same area to defend the wing player who just made the short-corner pass (02). When the ball is caught in the short-corner area, everyone then locks in to the man in his respective designated area and all five defenders now have man-to-man responsibilities (see Diagram 10.4).

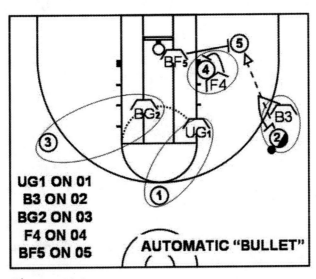

Diagram 10.4

The fifth method of defending the short-corner pass is to simply have all five defenders execute the standard down slide as if the down pass is made to a pass receiver in the deep corner (see Diagram 10.5). The main advantage of this defensive coverage is that all defenders should be very familiar with the down slide and no guessing or decision-making has to be made on the part of the back forward to determine whether the offensive pass receiver is in the short-corner area or in the deep-corner area. The disadvantages are that the original front man (F4) might have a poor angle to close out on the ball (05) as well as being able to close out quickly enough.

Having one or two of these fundamentally sound defensive options to defend against the zone offense's short-corner action is a necessity. After the coaching staff has determined which methods are the best methods for their particular defensive personnel, they must teach (with complete faith and confidence), drill, and sell their team on the fact that the match-up zone defense can successfully neutralize an opponent's offensive short-corner attack. The five given methods are integral parts of your defensive package. You can choose not only what is best for your personnel, but you can also choose whatever will best defend the opposition's personnel.

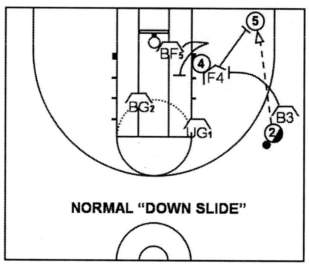

NORMAL "DOWN SLIDE"

Diagram 10.5

Versus Ball Screen Offensive Action

If ball screens are set for the point guard (O1) by a wing player (O2) near the top of the key, and the back guard (BG2) has no immediate coverage, he can help out the up guard (UG1) when he is screened. The back guard can step up and aggressively trap the dribbler with the up guard or he could switch with the up guard to pick up the dribbler and actually become the new up guard while the original up guard switches to become the next new back guard.

When the ball reaches the free-throw line extended, the ballhandler is then picked up on a true switch slide by the outside backline defender on the ballside (X3). On this slide, the newest up guard (X2) would drop back to the ballside elbow area and remain as the up guard, while the newest back guard (X1) would align in the proper stance and location as the current back guard (see Diagram 10.6).

If an offensive player is near the high-post area (O5) and he is the actual offensive player setting the ball screen for the point guard (O1), the first back guard (BG2) can again aggressively switch the ball screen (to become the new up guard). The original up guard (UG1) would then become the next back guard after the switch or the double-team trap on the ball screen. No other defenders would be involved in this defensive counterattack to specific types of offensive ball screens (see Diagram 10.7).

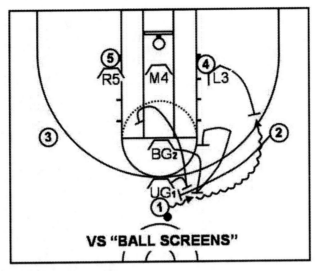

Diagram 10.6

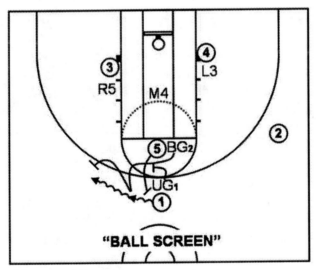

Diagram 10.7

If an opponent's ballside high-post player (05) steps out to ball screen the ballhandler (02) at the free-throw line extended, the current up guard (UG1) could step up and aggressively trap the ballhandler (02), or switch or hedge the screen and let the original defender (B3) stay with the ballhandler (see Diagram 10.8).

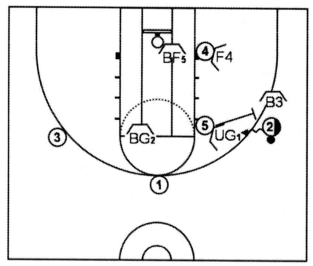

Diagram 10.8

Versus Weakside High- and Low-Post Action

This offensive action has to have been initiated on the opposite side away from the ballside action without ballside post players. An offensive player also has to be near the top of the key (03) to be able to continue the swing of the ball from the initial ballside to the weakside where the post players are located.

An open call will declare no ballside high-post player and an empty call will declare no ballside low-post player. Therefore, when the wing pass is made to the defense's left side (from 01 to 02) away from the two post players (04 and 05), the empty call allows the first front man (M4) to be in a pistols stance while straddling the ballside line in the lane. The back forward (BF5) straddles the manside line in the pistols stance. The open call allows the up guard (UG1) to be in a pistols stance while straddling the free-throw line at the ballside elbow and the back guard (BG2) can straddle the manside line level with the weakside high-post player (04) (see Diagram 10.9).

Since an open call is made, when the ball is reversed to the top of the key (from 02 to 01), the current up guard (UG1) should take the pass receiver (01) on the centered-up slide, which frees up the original back guard (BG2) to be able to remain as the back guard and cover the weakside high-post player (04). Because of his initial position and stance with the empty call, the original back forward (BF5) should be able to get on the outside and above the weakside low-post player (05) and not get pin screened in if the ball is continued on toward the wing on his side of the floor (to 03). Because of the empty call, the original front man (F4) should also get over and around the low post player on the new ballside (05) (see Diagram 10.10).

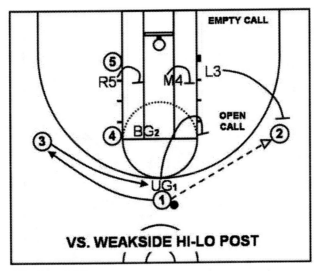

Diagram 10.9

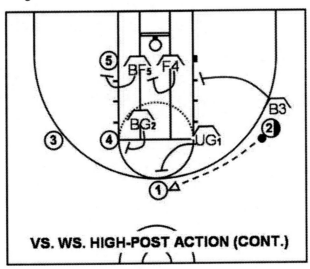

Diagram 10.10

When the ball is continued to the wing (O3) on the opposite side (the side where the two post players are located) , the first back forward (R5) closes out and becomes the new ball man and funnels the ball. The first front man (M4) is now the front man on the new ballside, while the original ball man (L3) becomes the new back forward.

The original up guard (UG1) remains the up guard on the first wing pass (to O2) and on the reversal pass (O1), but on the wing pass on the side of the high-post player (O3) he must become the next back guard. The original back guard (BG2) remains as the back guard shaded toward the offensive high-post player (O4). When the ball was passed to O3 on the side of the post players, BG2 stays there to cover that high-post opponent (O4) and becomes the next up guard (see Diagram 10.11).

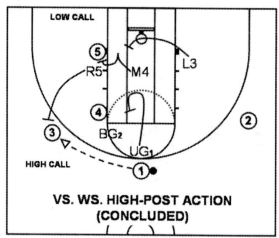

Diagram 10.11

Versus Pin Screen Offensive Action

The only players that could get pin screened would be the backline players on the outside of the match-up zone. These backline players must remember that they are in the match-up zone defense. While man-to-man defensive concepts and techniques (such as going ball screen on all off-the-ball screens) are very sound defensive concepts and could be effective in the match-up zone, the most effective method of defending pin screens while in the match-up zone is to closely follow the cutter on the manside of the pin screen. This defensive method should prevent any offensive flare cuts by the cutter (03) off of the pin screen (set by 05), which would be the biggest threat to the match-up zone defense (see Diagram 10.12).

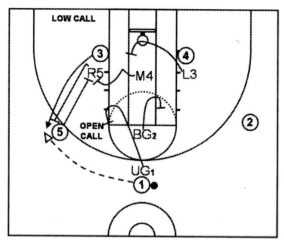

Diagram 10.12

If the offensive cutter, upon reading the defender going to the manside of the screen, curls back toward the basket, the match-up zone defense will always have built-in defensive support on the interior of the defense to negate that offensive action. Offensive flare cuts or fades (on the perimeter) are a bigger potential offensive threat to the match-up zone defense than the curl cuts are.

The original middle man (M4) must get to and then get around to completely front the offensive pin screener (05 in Diagram 10.12) who becomes the new offensive low post player. The defender in the middle (M4) becomes the new front man and uses the appropriate stance, location, and techniques that every front man in the match-up zone should use.

If the defender who is getting pin screened (R5 in Diagram 10.12) goes to the manside of the screen and then closely follows the offensive cutter (03) on his heels, he will not be able to deny the offensive wing (03) the ball. But by the time 03 catches the ball, pivots, and squares up to the basket, the defender should be able to closely guard the ball and discourage most perimeter shots and many passes that 03 could possibly make (see Diagram 10.12).

This offensive action can (and should) be neutralized fairly easily if the original up guard (UG1), the original back guard (BG2), the original back forward (BF3), and the original front man (F4) all utilize the proper TIPS—that is, the proper *techniques*, high *intensity* levels, correct *positioning*, and the correct *stance*.

It is important that the original up guard (UG1) remain as the up guard on the centered-up slide so that the back guard (BG2) can remain on the high-post player (04). It is also necessary for the original back forward (BF5) to respond to the ball reversal and to be able to place maximum pressure on 03 as the new ball man on the second wing pass (from 01 to 03). It is just as important that the original front man (F4) reacts to the reversal pass (from 02 to 01) and the second wing pass (from 01 to 03) so that he can effectively become the next front man on the opposite side of the floor.

Versus Two-Guard Front Offensive Sets

A natural counter move by the opposition's offense is to align in a two-guard front versus the 0 zone that incorporates the 1-1-3 defensive alignment. An easy and simple defensive counter move to the opposition's offensive plan is to simply rotate the up guard (UG1) and the back guard (BG2) from a vertical tandem to a horizontal tandem. The 0 zone then transforms into the 2 zone.

If the offense brings a player up to the high-post area, the defense should simply walk up the original middle man (M4) to play behind the offensive high-post player

(05). The offensive post player (05) is too far from the basket, so he would not be side or completely fronted (as he would in the side high-post or low-post areas). If the offensive post player receives the ball from one of the two guards, M4 would then pressure the ball, while the up guard (UG1) and the back guard (BG2) would collapse on 05 behind his line of sight to discourage any high-post offensive action (see Diagram 10.13).

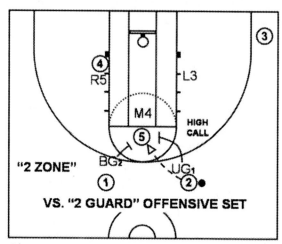

Diagram 10.13

If the ball is down-passed from the two-guard front to the baseline corner (from 02 to 03), the match-up zone still provides a new ball man (L3 in Diagram 10.14) to be able to easily close out on the ballhandler (03). The original middle man (M4) uses the man-to-man defensive concept of jumping to the ball so that he can quickly utilize the proper stance and technique in the proper location as the defense's new front man (see Diagram 10.14).

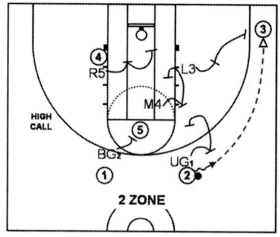

Diagram 10.14

Diagram 10.15 illustrates the proper locations of all five defenders in the match-up zone on the down pass out of a two-guard offensive front. On the down pass from 02 to 03, the offense often will have its high-post player (05) slide down the lane and post up on the new ballside low post. If that offensive action takes place, BF5 should provide for some instant relief in the (new) ballside low-post area as F4 jumps to the ball on the down pass and not only beats the opposition's high-post player to the low-post spot but also hinders his progress and then completely fronts the new low-post player (05). BF5 then drops off and becomes the true back forward while B3 remains the defense's true ball man (see Diagram 10.15). The offense, upon seeing the defense's middle man pulled up to the high post, could counter this defensive move with a different offensive player (04) flashing to the new ballside low-post area, hoping to beat the front man (F4) to the spot.

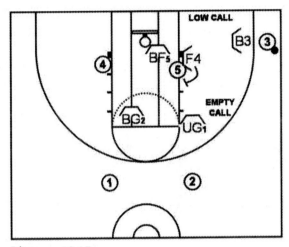

Diagram 10.15

Diagram 10.16 illustrates the defensive adjustment. The baseline defender in the 2 zone on the weakside would be R5 and when 04 flashes across the lane, R5 should challenge the cut and actually become the match-up zone's new front man on the ballside block. When the original up guard quickly drops down to cover the ballside high post, F4 instantly drops down to become the defense's new back forward to provide helpside support for the new front man (F5) (see Diagram 10.16).

The second option of defending an opposition's offense that incorporates a two-guard front can be implemented with a standard stunt that would automatically be executed on any down pass that comes from a two-guard offensive set. Diagram 10.17 shows an example of how the match-up zone defense adjusts to become the 2 zone, with the up guard (UG1) and the back guard (BG2) aligning in a horizontal tandem and the middle man (M4) moving up to the free-throw line to play behind the offense's high-post player (05), leaving two backline defenders (R5 and L3) just outside the lane near the low-post area on their side of the floor.

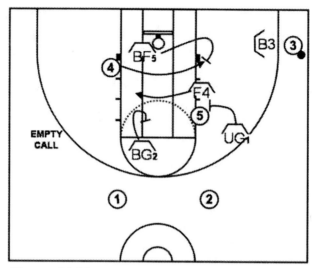

Diagram 10.16

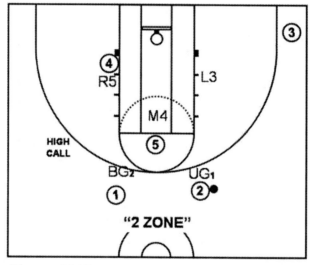

Diagram 10.17

Diagram 10.18 illustrates the example of 02 down-passing the ball to the baseline to 03 on the defense's left side of the floor. This down pass activates the bullet stunt and all five defenders pick up the appropriate offensive opponent located in or near his designated area. The defender on the (left side's) backline (L3) on the ballside must close out on the ball in the corner and then stay with that player (03). The original middle man (M4) drops to become the front man unless an offensive player other than the original high-post player (such as 04) flashes to the new ballside low post. If an offensive player (other than the original high-post player) flashes across the lane to the ballside low-post area, R5 would disrupt that flash post cut and stay with that man (04). As stated upon the first down pass, all five defenders should match up to the appropriate offensive player in his general area and stay with that player in a man-to-man defensive concept. The up guard (UG1) and the back guard (BG2) literally match up with the opponents in their respective areas (02 and 01, respectively).

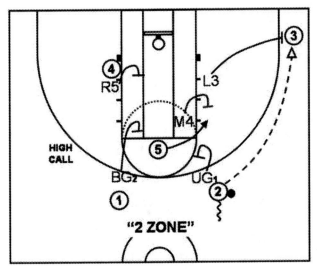

Diagram 10.18

Diagram 10.19 illustrates a two-guard offensive alignment with a high-post player at the free-throw line (05). This scheme has a weakside offensive player (04) flash across the lane to the new ballside low post and the original ballside high-post player remains at the high post. Upon the first down pass (from 02 to 03), L3 should close out and stay on that opponent. M4 stays with 05, and R5 goes across the lane to defend 04 on his low-post flash. UG1 and BG2 match up to the guards above the free-throw line extended and remain there.

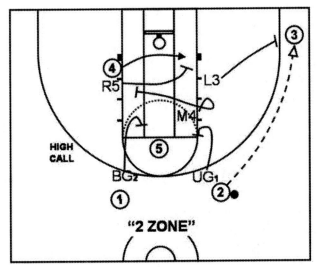

Diagram 10.19

Diagram 10.20 shows the defensive action when an opposition's offense makes the down pass (to 03), has 05 slide down to the new ballside low-post area, and then has the weakside low-post player (04) flash to the newly-vacated ballside high-post area. The opposition also has the passing guard (02) exchange with 01 out on top. In this scenario, L3 picks up and stays on 03 in the corner, M4 remains on 05 in the low-post area, R5 stays with 04 at the ballside high post, UG1 picks up 01, and BG2 now defends 02.

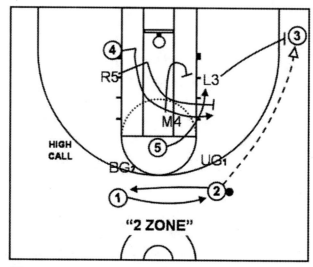

Diagram 10.20

With the defense beginning in one of the odd-front match-up zones (either the 0 zone or the 3 zone), it is very logical for an offensive opponent to react to the defense and make an adjustment to a different offense. That change could very well be an offensive adjustment into an offensive two-guard front. With the defense able to easily and confidently change to the 2 zone, the defense once again has become actors and forced the opposition to become reactors. The 2 zone has the capability to neutralize the offensive scheme and plan of attack. Being in the 2 zone versus an offensive two-guard front should make it easier for the defensive team to succeed and then possibly force the opposition back into an odd front zone offense. When that happens, the defense counters by going back to the 0 zone.

Versus Double High-Post Alignments

Sometimes an opposing team will align their offensive team in a 1-4 high alignment. This alignment allows the up guard (UG1) to match up to the offense's point guard (01), but overloads the back guard (BG2) with two different high-post players to defend (04 and 05).

This offensive alignment causes the offense to outnumber the defensive front of two defenders (to defend against the five offensive players that are at or above the free-throw line extended). The easiest method to discourage this offensive set is to walk the two outside defenders (R5 and L3) up and place them slightly below and shaded on the outside shoulder of the high-post player on their side. The middle man (M4) stays in his usual stance at his (0-zone) location in the middle of the lane slightly above the blocks (see Diagram 10.21).

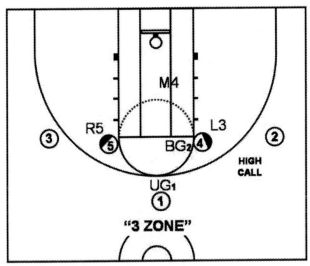

Diagram 10.21

When the wing pass is made from 01 to 02, L3 must quickly execute the wing slide by closing out on the ball in the normal outside-in angle to funnel the basketball. The funnel overplay position of the new ball man (L3) is the same in the 3 zone as it is in the 0 zone. Whether it is the original up guard (UG1) or the back guard (BG2) that is the first defender that can get to the new ballside high post (04), that defender (BG2) should front the top half of the ballside high-post player (04). A high call should be made. The up guard should be in the pistols stance at the ballside line if an open call is made and no ballside high-post player is utilized. The other defender should become the new back guard and he should be in the usual pistols stance at the manside line when an open call is made. If a high call is made, he should remain in the pistols stance but should be located at the manside line.

The middle man (M4) jumps to the ball when the wing pass is made (from 01 to 02) and quickly gets in his pistols stance straddling the free-throw-lane line near the medium low-post area on the new ballside (An empty call is made). He is prepared to defend any flash post players coming anywhere from the new ballside or from the weakside.

When that wing pass is made to L3's side of the floor, R5 would immediately become the first back forward by also jumping to the ball. He should get in his usual off-the-ball pistols stance and straddle the manside line only if an empty call is made. If a low call is made, the new back forward (BF5) should straddle the ballside line in his pistols stance.

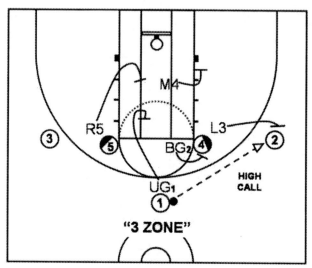

Diagram 10.22

This defensive adjustment of simply moving two defenders (and aligning in the 3-zone defensive alignment) discourages the offense from passing the ball directly to either high-post player (05 or 04). If the ball is passed to either wing (03 or 02), that particular defender can easily close out and get in the proper position to funnel the ball back towards the middle.

The defense has taken on a completely different appearance, but the change is only cosmetic. While appearing to now be in a 1-3-1 zone defense, the defenders are actually now in the 3 match-up zone. Every defensive slide of the 3 zone is the same as the 0 zone and only X3 and X5 have changed their initial location.

All coverage responsibilities, all defensive box-out responsibilities, and all stunts of the 0 zone can be incorporated in the 3 zone. To the defensive team, the only difference between the 0 zone and the 3 zone is the initial position of L3 and R5, but to the opposition, a completely different defense seems to be employed.

Changing from the 0 zone to the 3 zone not only improves the coverage protection of all defenders, but can also confuse the opposition into thinking the entire defensive scheme and attitude has changed (when in fact, it has not). Many times, the opposition will then change their zone offensive attack when they see the defense change to what appears to them to be a typical 1-3-1 zone. The action of the defense could then cause the offense to react and change again by switching to the 3-zone alignment (with the same basic slides and responsibilities as the 0 zone) or by implementing one of the stunts of the multiple match-up zone out of the 3-zone alignment. These stunts out of the 3 zone should not in any way mentally overtax the defenders.

11

Evaluation of the Multiple Match-Up Zone Defense and the Implemented Stunts

If the coaching staff chooses to run any of the various stunts that are available, a statistics chart is strongly recommended to evaluate the performance and the efficiency of each stunt, as well as that of the overall defense. Each stunt should be charted as to the total number of defensive possessions for each stunt, the total number of points that were scored during those possessions, the numbers of all made and attempted shots (such as the inside shots, outside shots, three-point shots, and the opposition's number of stickback shots), the number of free-throw trips, the total number of turnovers committed by the opposition, the total number of offensive rebounds by the opposition, and the number of defensive rebounds by the defending team.

Dividing the total points by the total number of possessions will give the coaching staff what is called the Defensive Efficiency Rating (DER). Dividing the number of the defensive team's defensive rebounds by the total number of shots missed by the opposition gives a statistic called the Defensive Rebounding Frequency (DRF). Dividing the number of the opponent's offensive rebounds by the total number of shots missed by the opposition gives a statistic called the Offensive Rebounding Frequency (ORF).

Calculating the DRF for the defensive team and the opponent's ORF allows you to compare stats with one stunt to the others, as well as the overall base defense. These stats can be compared from one game to every other game, as well as from one season to other seasons. Since boxing out, opponent's offensive rebounding, and defensive rebounding are always of great concern, those statistics are then created, studied, and evaluated.

This stat-keeping is even more important for the coaching staff that elects to implement more than one of the three different defenses in the same season. These same statistics must be kept during games for that coach to decide which match-up zone is the most effective and productive for that particular quarter of play, or for that game.

If the defensive team can physically and mentally handle using multiple defenses and/or stunts, it is extremely difficult for an opponent to scout and prepare to play against a team that utilizes multiple match-up defenses. As a defensive team early in the game probes the opponent's offense for weaknesses without getting hurt defensively, it can cause more unrest for the opposition.

When a specific defense discovers offensive weaknesses and then attacks those weaknesses, it can be the difference in winning or losing a game. Stats are then essential in allowing a head coach to make the right decision in how to not only defend the opponent, but aggressively attack the opponent's offense. By choosing the correct stunts or the actual best defense, the multiple match-up zone defense can definitely be the margin of victory in many games.

Figure 11.1 is an example of a chart you can use to record each possession and what happens in that possession. These stats allow you to obtain the previously mentioned ratios. It is easy to evaluate your results. The lower the DER, the better the defense being used. You can even evaluate at halftime and use the best defense more often during the second half of the game, or during any crucial time of the game.

Opponent:	Date:	Quarter:	Zone:
Name of Stunt	Points Scored	Possessions	Points per Possession
Hard			
Jump			
Double			
Hard-Jump Combo			
Jump-Double Combo			
Smash			
Double-Smash			
Read			
Double-Read			
Choke			
Double-Choke			
Lock			
Left Lock			
Right Lock			
Bullet			
Left Bullet			
Right Bullet			
Totals	Points	Possessions	Points per Possession

Figure 11.1

12

Breakdown Drills

Many techniques must be properly performed by each and every individual player for the overall match-up defense to be successful. Players must be thoroughly taught and then coached via hours of teaching and repetition drills in practice. Practice time is limited but the amount of teaching and coaching is unlimited. Therefore, practice is extremely important and the budgeting of time is of vital importance to a coaching staff. Following is a brief coaching philosophy on practices that should be very important to every coaching staff:

- Coaches must thoroughly know the subject matter that they are presenting.
- Coaches must be enthusiastic and operate at a high energy level.
- Coaches should use the whole-part-whole teaching method when teaching players something new.
- Coaches must thoroughly and consistently sell the importance of those techniques to every player.
- Drills must be carefully developed and created by the coaching staff to teach and refine those techniques.
- The coaching staff must devise drills that will be game-realistic so that players will have the opportunity to learn and then practice those techniques in a setting that is as close to an actual game as possible.
- Coaches must develop a detailed practice plan. It must be carefully thought out before practice and then followed as closely as possible. The old adage, "Plan your work and then work your plan," is sound coaching advice.

- Coaches must be a stickler for details.
- Players' attention, concentration level, and effort must not be requested by the coaching staff, but demanded. Players will operate and practice at the level that the coaching staff allows them to practice.
- Coaching staffs should make drills more demanding and tougher than actual game situations.
- Coaches should not allow a drill to last too long, because the concentration level of everyone can decrease and make the time wasted. If the technique requires a great deal of time, work on the drill for just a few minutes and move to something else. Coaches can then come back to the drill for a few minutes and repeat as often as needed.
- Coaching staffs should make sure that drills include transition from offense to defense and from defense to offense.

In addition to drills with the entire defensive team working together, other drills can and should be broken down in smaller groups. Drills can be broken down into two groups of players: the match-up zone defense's frontline players and the backline players. Each of those groups should work on the following types of techniques:
- Proper positioning/location and stances
- Communication
- Slides
- Defensive box-outs and rebounds
- Transition from defense to offense and from offense to defense.

All drills should be practiced on both the left and the right sides of the court with many repetitions, with the coaching staff being very observant of all of the small details in the players' various positions/locations, stances, and the many techniques needed for the overall defense to be successful. The smallest of details should be observed, evaluated, and corrected constantly.

Coverage Drill

Diagrams 12.1 through 12.3 show breakdown drills that can be used to emphasize the proper positioning and the proper stances of all five defenders, to emphasize communication between all five defenders, and to emphasize the proper execution of the wing slide and the centered-up slide.

Six offensive players are in each diagram. Overloading the defense in practice situations ideally makes the defense better for games. If the five defenders can prevent the six attackers from getting a shot off, the defense is ready for any five-on-five play.

Diagram 12.1 shows UG1 guarding O1, who has the basketball. BG2 takes the high post. Because players are in both low posts, L3 opens on the left low post and R5 opens on the right low post. M4 defends the middle lane.

Diagram 12.2 displays the coverage when a high-post player is on the defense's left side, and Diagram 12.3 exhibits the coverage when a high-post player is on the defense's right side.

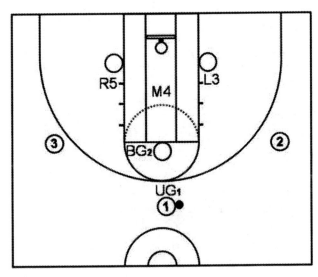

Diagram 12.1

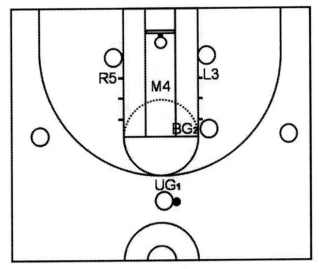

Diagram 12.2

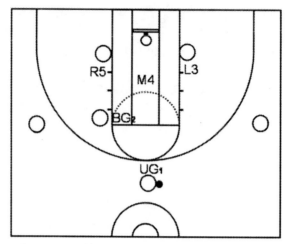

Diagram 12.3

You should begin this drill by allowing only passing (and no shooting or driving) between the offensive players. Each attacker should hold the ball for a few seconds before passing on the next attacker. The defenders slide to cover the proper attacker. After you are content with the slides, you allow the attackers to try to get shots off from a stationary position. If the defenders can stop a shot attempt, they have learned their slides well and the defense is ready for game competition.

Diagram 12.4 shows one of the options in defending the pass to the short corner. The proper slides and techniques, as well as the positioning of all five defenders, should be worked on by all players and corrected by the coaching staff. Only five offensive players are in this drill. Diagram 12.4 begins with the proper coverage when the ball is at the left wing.

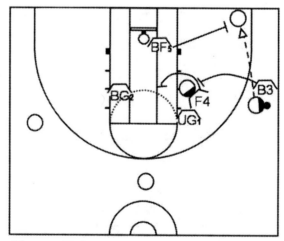

Diagram 12.4

Rotation Drill

Diagram 12.5 illustrates the proper two-man rotation of the down slide after the offense's down pass is made on the right side of the court. Down passes on both sides of the court should be practiced and worked on.

Shell Drill (Cutter's)

Diagram 12.6 illustrates a drill where the slide resulting from a wing pass is worked on and how defenders can work on communication of offensive players making the various cuts toward the ball to different positions on the floor—such as the ballside low post, the short corner, the deep corner, and the ballside high post. The techniques of how certain defenders should defend the high-post and low-post flash cuts are also worked on. L3 picks up the wing, 02. Players 06, 07, and 08 all make cuts into the middle of the defense—one goes to short corner, one to low post, and one to side high post. BG2, M4, and R5 must communicate and make the proper coverage.

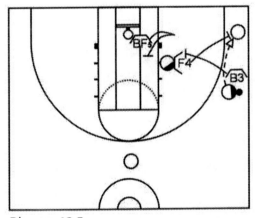

Diagram 12.5

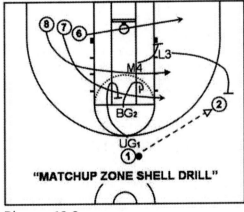

Diagram 12.6

Diagram 12.7 illustrates a drill where the down pass is made by the offense and ways in which defenders can work on calling out the various cuts by the offensive opponents to the various positions on the court. Notice that although the diagram is set up on the defense's right side of the court, this drill (and all drills) should be practiced on both sides. Techniques of how to see and call out to warn defensive teammates and how certain defenders should defend the high-post and low-post flash cuts are also worked on.

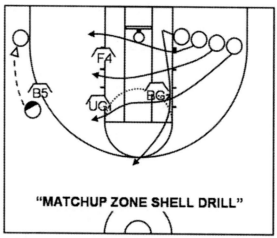

"MATCHUP ZONE SHELL DRILL"

Diagram 12.7

Transition Drills
(Defense-to-Offense and Offense-to-Defense)

From the shell drill, a defensive-to-offensive transition drill can be implemented. This drill allows the defensive team to be able to work on its primary and secondary fastbreaks immediately out of the match-up zone defense (see Diagram 12.8).

Another drill, the offensive-to-defensive transition drill, has the team in a controlled half-court offensive setting against a dummy defense. On a designated call, the offensive team drops the ball to allow the dummy defense to start their fastbreak. The offensive team must then sprint back to first stop the fastbreak before setting up the match-up zone defense to then begin the match-up zone shell drill.

The Match-Up Zone Shell Drill

This variation of a man-to-man defensive shell drill was created to help improve defensive players' positioning and stances. Offensive players are placed in

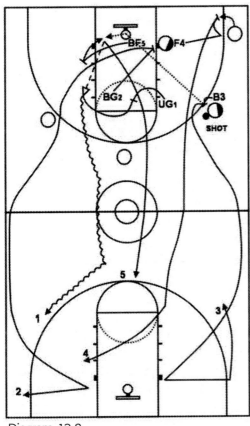

Diagram 12.8

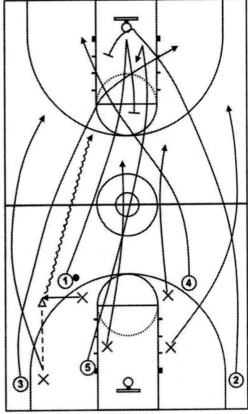

Diagram 12.9

predesignated spots so zone defenders will learn the proper slides for covering offensive opponents in those areas. The dummy offense in this drill is very much restricted so that all of the attention can be devoted to the defensive part of the drill (see Diagram 12.9).

Match-Up Super Shell Drill

The match-up super shell drill utilizes the overload theory with nine offensive players for the five match-up zone players to defend. The nine offensive players are in somewhat of a controlled setting in that each offensive player is restricted so that he can only take two dribbles. After catching the ball, each offensive player must square up to the basket and wait for two counts before then passing the ball. The ball must be dribbled or passed and cannot be shot. The proper positioning, stances, and techniques are constantly observed and evaluated (see Diagram 12.10). After some time, the defensive-to-offensive transition can be added to the drill to make it also a transition drill.

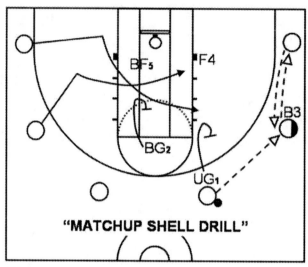

"MATCHUP SHELL DRILL"

Diagram 12.10

A different version of the match-up shell drill is to have six or seven offensive players aligned in various spots on the perimeter. As the ball is passed around, offensive players on the weakside should flash to the low post and the high post on the ballside. When the ball is passed around and no post players are hit with the pass, the post players empty out and go back to their original perimeter positions. When the ball is swung to their side, the perimeter players on the opposite side make unpredictable flashes to the low post and the high post. This drill continues the work on defensive positioning, stances, slides, and communication (see Diagram 12.11).

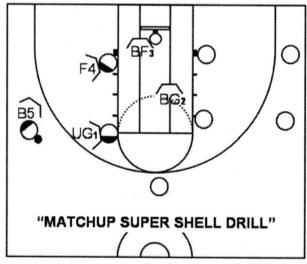

"MATCHUP SUPER SHELL DRILL"

Diagram 12.11

Match-Up Box-Out and Fast Break Drill

This drill is used to work on the defensive box-outs while offensive players are placed in the many various offensive positions so that each defender can work on his particular box-out priority list. After each defender decides the appropriate area to prioritize his defensive box-out, the actual box-out techniques are practiced, as well as the actual techniques of the defensive rebound and outlet passes to initiate transition fastbreaks. Added to the drill later could be primary fastbreak and secondary fastbreak after the defensive rebound and outlet passes.

In addition to working on the defensive box-outs, the defensive rebounds, the outlet passes, and the transition from defense to offense, this drill can be used to practice the primary and secondary fastbreaks from the defensive half court to the offensive end at the opposite end of the floor (see Diagram 12.12).

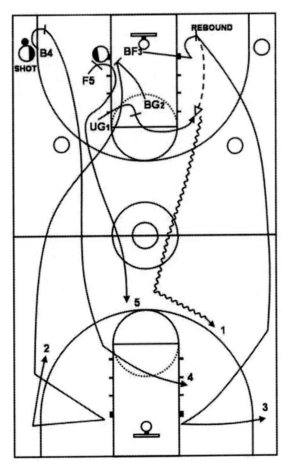

Diagram 12.12

Man-to-Man Defensive Breakdown Drills

Several defensive stunts (such as left bullet, right bullet, bullet, left lock, right lock, and lock) transform the match-up zone defense into a man-to-man defense, at least for the one possession. It is therefore necessary (and obvious) that many man-to-man defensive breakdown drills should be incorporated in the daily practice sessions to make the match-up zone defense an effective and successful defense. Two of the most important breakdown drills that are used in teaching and improving the man-to-man defenses are the pride drill and the team shell drill.

Pride Drill

The pride drill (see Diagram 12.13) can predominantly be an individual man-to-man defensive drill that works on defensive techniques and skills. In addition, the drill develops a tough hard-nosed attitude for every defensive player, as well as establishes a high intensity level for each player. With the physical and mental effort that this drill

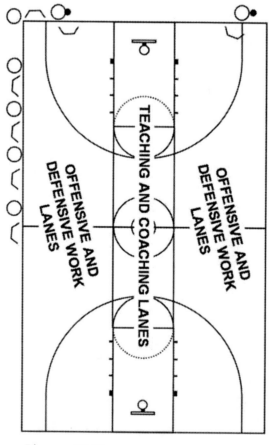

Diagram 12.13

requires, it also becomes a great conditioning drill. Offensive fundamental work can be incorporated into the drill to add offensive work and additional intensity for both the offense and the defense.

Some of the offensive techniques that can be worked on are the various types of dribbling, screens, cuts, passes, and other offensive fundamentals. The dribbles used are behind-the-back dribbling, between-the-leg dribbling, and front-crossover dribbling. The proper techniques of all of the offensive fundamentals should be a part of this drill.

The drill is started with offensive restrictions for two important reasons. One reason is to allow the defense an opportunity to succeed before making the drill more difficult (and more game-realistic) as the defenders progress in developing skills and building confidence. The second reason for giving offensive restrictions is to force the offensive players into working on any specific ballhandling techniques for which the coaching staff feels that either the team or individuals need to improve.

One way of making the drill more difficult (and, therefore, more game-realistic) is to lengthen and widen the dribbling area. At the beginning of this drill, the area can be shortened and narrowed to promote success for the defenders. As the defenders master the skills and techniques, the drill can be made more challenging and game-realistic by expanding the offensive dribbling area. Using the overload theory in all drills make the drills as physically and mentally tough as possible to simulate game realism and also go at game speed.

When the drill can be advanced to using the full length of the court, it can then be expanded into the many different defensive techniques being applied during the course of the pride drill. Some of the defensive techniques that can be worked on and emphasized in the pride drill are:
- Taking the charge
- Defending a killed dribbler
- Defending a cutter (on a give-and-go situation)
- Boxing out a shooter (off of the dribble)
- Recovering after the dribbler has beaten the defender
- Diving for loose balls
- Closing out on a potential driver/jump-shooter
- Defending against an on-the-ball screen
- Defending against an off-the-ball screen
- Helping out on a teammate's man and then recovering onto his own man
- Sprinting out of a trap situation onto his own man
- Wolf deflecting from behind and getting ahead of the dribbler

- Defending (and pressuring) a killed dribbler
- Jump-switching onto the new dribbler

These (and other) defensive scenarios can be practiced at the very beginning and at the very end of the dribbling area. Different situations can be used every time at the beginning and at the end of each offensive trip down the lane both offensively, as well as defensively. Some of the offensive scenarios that defensive or offensive players can work on at the beginning of the offensive trips include:
- Receiving a standard pass
- Receiving off-the-ball screens before receiving the pass
- Shot-faking after receiving the pass, but before starting the dribble-drive
- Receiving ball screens after receiving a pass

During the offensive trip, the dribbler may be asked to work on a specific type of dribble, or a pass to a coach and then running a specific cut. At the end of the offensive trip, the dribbler may be required to shoot the ball, charge into the defender, kill the dribble, or roll the ball across the floor (to simulate a loose ball fumble).

Following is an example of the different defensive trips that your team can work on. Different combinations should be used daily, which will help the players learn to carefully listen and follow instructions precisely—both offensively and defensively.

On the first trip down the court, the dribbler and the defender can create a situation where the defense must defend the new dribbler after he has received a (make-believe) skip pass. The defender starts in a pistols stance and then closes out on the new dribbler. The defender now zigzags down the dribbling area until the dribbler gets to the end of the lane, where the defender then draws an offensive charge on the dribbler.

The dribbler can simply put the ball into the chest of the defender to establish the physical contact required to initiate the offensive foul. No additional physical contact has to occur between the two players, thus decreasing the risks of injuries to either participating player. When the ball has made the contact with the defender, he pushes off on his heels and falls to the floor. In drawing the charge, the following points of emphasis should be stressed to the players:
- Protect the groin and chest area by locking your arms in front of those two areas.
- Push off backward with the heels at the exact moment of contact.
- Tuck the chin.
- Try to slide on the tail on the floor.
- Raise the legs up into the chest area to protect from the offensive player landing on the defender.
- Grunt out an "ugh!" to help the official make the charging call.

The drill then continues with a new pair of players. Coaches should have the offensive player help the defender up after taking the charge. The first pair of players go to the end of the line and switch defensive-offensive roles (see Diagram 12.14).

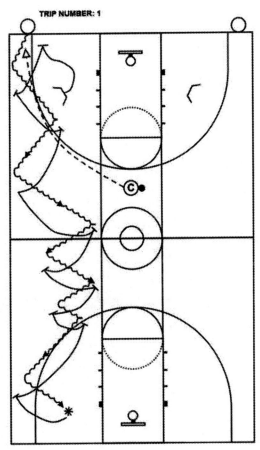

Diagram 12.14

The second trip could begin with the main defender starting as a one-pass-away off-the-ball defender. The dummy dribbler should dribble into the gap if the two defenders. The main defender then *helps* (to stop penetration) and *recovers* to his original man as his offensive opponent receives the pass. From there, the defender uses the proper push-push-push and drop step techniques as he zigzags down the dribbling alley. When the dribbler reaches the far baseline, he kills his dribble. This action causes the defender to defend a killed dribbler. Major points in defending a killed dribbler include:

- Step up hard into the killed dribbler and force the potential passer to put the ball over his head or to turn away from the hard defensive pressure that is being applied. Doing so takes away the majority of the potential pass receivers that the passer has (remember, the passer has only five seconds to find that open receiver and make the pass to him).

- Cross-face with the hands and prevent the passer from bringing the ball back down to waist or chest level.
- Coaches should have the defender yell, "Work! Work!" and pressure the passer as much as possible (see Diagram 12.15).

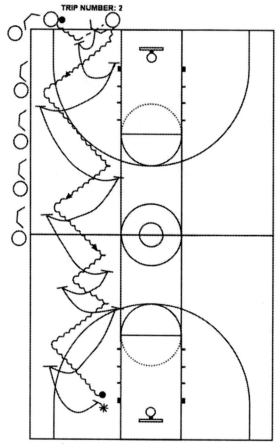

Diagram 12.15

On the third trip down the defensive lane, the defender is still working on the proper ball defender's techniques with his feet and his hands. The proper stance and push technique of the feet and legs should be stressed. The dig hand and the extended hand and arm techniques are constantly reinforced. The third trip can be initiated with one or two dummy screeners ball screening the defender. The defender must feel for the screen and go over the top (ballside of the screen) and hustle to stay or get ahead of the dribbler. The zigzagging action would then continue.

After turning the dribbler several times down the dribbling alley, the dribbler passes the ball to a coach or manager who is standing near the far free-throw line. As soon as that pass is made, the dribbler-passer becomes a cutter-receiver. He makes a very hard give-and-go cut toward the end of the alley. The defender has to defend against a receiver (instead of a dribbler). The defender should jump to the ball and match hands and belly buttons. He should yell, "Help," snap his head, and look down his longarm (i.e., the arm that is extended near the offensive player) in an attempt to see the ball and his man. The dummy passer should force a pass to the give-and-go cutter, resulting in a completion, a pass deflection, or an interception (see Diagram 12.16).

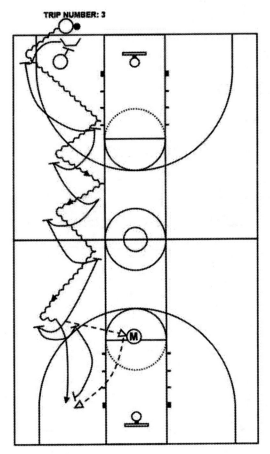

Diagram 12.16

The fourth trip could start with an off-the-ball screen on the original defender. He should go ballside of the screen, turn sideways to get skinny (in an attempt to avoid the screen), and slide through with a long arm towards the potential offensive receiver. The defender should go full speed but allow the pass to be made. Once the pass is completed, the dribbling and the defensive zigzagging starts again down the dribbling alley. At the end of the fourth trip, the dribbler jumps and shoots the ball at an imaginary basket several feet in front of him (to simulate a jump shot off of the dribble) (see Diagram 12.17). The defender defends against the shot by:

- Not leaving the ground until the shooter leaves the ground
- Extending the hand (nearest the ball) and arm as high as possible
- Front-pivoting into the shooter and boxing out the shooter. The defender should maintain contact on the shooter for three seconds before quitting.

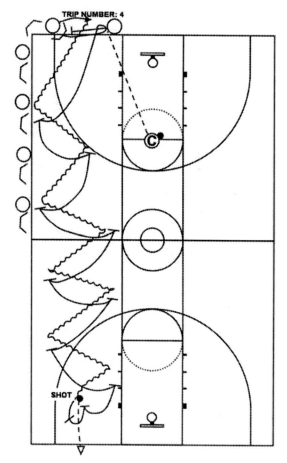

Diagram 12.17

Cardinal rules that a good defensive system should incorporate for all of its individual defenders on the shooter include:

- Do not foul a jump-shooter.
- Do not leave the ground until the shooter leaves the ground.
- Do not give the shooter a second scoring opportunity.

On the fifth trip down the floor, the dribbler is allowed a two-step advantage on the defender. The defender must realize that he is beaten, pivot, open up, get the correct pursuit angle, and sprint to a spot ahead of the advancing dribbler. He then must get in front of the dribbler and be squared up on him, knowing that the dribbler will then most likely try to change directions. He should anticipate another defensive change of direction.

The teaching phrase used at this point is to tell the defense they are there physically, but mentally they are already drop-stepping toward the new direction by the dribbler. The dribbler then continues zigzagging down toward the far baseline. At the end of the trip, the dribbler has again been forced to kill his dribble. When that happens, the dribbler, simulating a loose ball, rolls out a ball for the defender to dive after (see Diagram 12.18).

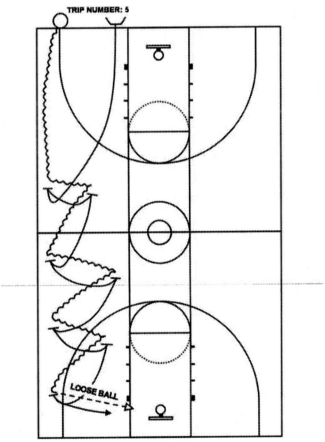

Diagram 12.18

Obviously, this defensive-minded drill requires effort from all of the players as well as the coaches. But the drill can be enhanced by having the dribbler working with both hands on the various types of dribbles the coaching staff allows. The head should stay up, with the body in a semi-crouch, dribbling quickly (but not in a hurry).

Any or all of the following dribbles could be used:
- Front crossover
- Between-the-legs dribble
- Behind-the-back dribble
- Reverse or spin dribble

The coaching staff could instruct the dribblers to use specific dribbles (or a combination of dribbles) to work on offensive improvement.

Starting Positions of the Pride Drill

- Positioning
- Closeout from a skip-pass
- Downscreen
- Ball screen
- Help-and-recover
- From a beaten position
- 55 soft defensive action
- Jump switch action
- Sprint out of trap to the dribbler
- "Wolf! Wolf!" to become a container
- From a stalker to become a container

Finishing Situations of the Pride Drill

- Box out a shooter
- Versus a give-and-go cutter
- Dive for a loose ball
- "Work! Work!" on a killed dribbler
- Take the charge
- Trap a new receiver
- Live one-on-one action (Scenario #1: The dribbler must zigzag and finally force the defense into the paint and then shoot the ball. He must then get an offensive rebound for a stickback. When the defender gets the defensive rebound, he then must outlet the ball via a dribble, until the new defender turns him at least one time.)
- Live one-on-one action (Scenario #2: The offensive dribbler must try to beat the defender, using both boundary lines, regardless of how wide or narrow they are. The dribbler should use both hands, with his head constantly up, looking at the rim. He should be using the various types of dribbles that the coaching staff wants him to work on.)

Countless combinations of starting and ending situations can be utilized. Mixing these combinations up helps eliminate boredom and complacency of the players. They are forced to listen and concentrate on remembering the many different defensive scenarios that the coaching staff lays out for them.

Team Shell Drill

This drill has numerous components that are used to teach and practice the proper defensive techniques required for a defensive team to be successful in its man-to-man defensive efforts. Following are offensive concepts that can (and should) be utilized during the team shell drill to make the man-to-man defense a very effective defense, as well as to make specific match-up zone defense stunts more effective.

Offensive Concepts and Scenarios

- Positioning
- Versus give-and-go cuts
- Versus backdoor cuts
- Versus clear-outs
- Versus skip passes
- Versus killed dribble
- Versus on-the-ball screens
- Versus off-the-ball down and cross screens
- Versus off-the-ball flare screens
- Versus off-the-ball back screens
- Versus off-the-ball flex back screens
- Versus off-the-ball shuffle-cut back screens
- Versus shuffle-cut action
- Versus wheel-cut action
- Versus scissor-cut action off of post
- Versus UCLA rub-off back screens
- Versus off-the-ball pin screens
- Versus off-the-ball stagger screens
- Versus off-the-ball lane-exchange screens
- Versus flash-post action
- Versus help-and-recover (G to G)
- Versus help-and-recover (G to F)
- Versus help-and-recover (G to C)
- Versus baseline drives
- Box-outs on a shooter

Daily use of the team shell drill, as well as continued emphasis on and utilization of the pride drill, will make a defensive team more than proficient in playing a solid man-to-man defense. Keeping every player involved, varying the different aspects (and rapidly changing from one to another), and staying with that aspect only for very small periods of time keep the players' focus at high levels. This approach keeps the intensity level up, which makes the drill productive and very time efficient for each individual, as well as for the team.

Basic Match-up Zone Breakdown Drills

In addition to the drills outlined earlier in this chapter, the following two basic match-up zone breakdown drills should be utilized to help improve the overall effectiveness of the team defense.

Backcourt Match-Up Drill

Diagram 12.19 shows six offensive players against two defenders. The drill begins with 01 in possession of the ball. In Diagram 12.19, 01 passes to 02, but 01 could pass to 02, 03, 05, or 06. The initial part of the drill does not allow shooting or dribbling. You are just working on the slides of UG1 and BG2. (As discussed in Chapter 6 , neither UG1 nor BG2 would cover this first pass to 02 or 03. It would be covered by L3 or R4, frontcourt defenders, and is not part of this drill). Player 02 can pass to either 03, 04, or back to 01. Again, the slides are the major point of emphasis.

After you are satisfied with the slides of the two defenders, you advance the drill by allowing any of the four attackers (01, 02, 03, and 04) to shoot the ball. If the two

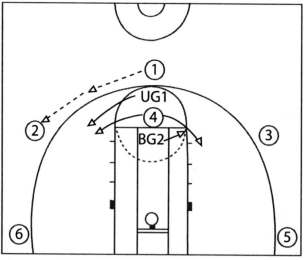

Diagram 12.19

guards can keep the attackers from getting a shot off, the two guards are ready for game action. The next progression of the drill is to allow the pass receiver to dribble the ball in any direction one or two dribbles.

The last progression is to enter O5 and O6. These two players are never allowed to shoot or dribble. They only pass the ball back out to the wing on their side of the court, to the point guard, or to the opposite wing. Because the slides and stances of UG1 and BG2 are different when the ball is in the corner, you need to add corner passers. With this addition, all possibilities of slides and stances will have been drilled.

Frontcourt Match-Up Drill

Diagrams 12.20 through 12.22 exhibit all the possible slides and stances of the frontcourt players—L3, M4, and R5. Diagram 12.20 shows the structure: six offensive players and only three defenders. A wing attacker (O1) begins with the ball. Player O1 can pass to O2, O3, O4, O5, or O6. The defenders must react with the proper slides and stances. In the beginning, you do not let any player shoot or dribble the basketball. Each new pass receiver holds the ball for a count of two and then passes it on. After the players have mastered the slides, you may allow quick movement of the ball. Now, the defenders still use the same slides and stances, they just have to react quicker.

In Diagram 12.20, O1 passes to O3. L3 and M4 execute the two-man rotation slide of the match-up zone. Now O3 can pass to any of the other five players except O1. A pass back to O1 would be covered by UG1, a backcourt defender (not used in this drill).

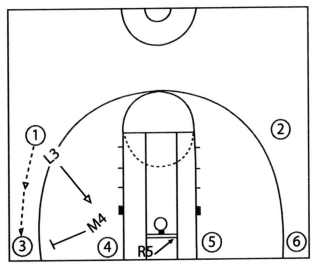

Diagram 12.20

Diagram 12.21 displays 03 skip passing to 02. It is R5's assignment to get to 02 before he can get a shot off. L3 and M4 execute their slides. Player 02 continues the drill by passing down to 06 (see Diagram 12.22). Players R5 and L3 execute the two-man rotation slide of the match-up zone. This sequence of passing continues with 06 skip passing to 01. Player 06 can pass to anyone except for 02. A pass back to 02 would be defended by either UG1 or BG2, both backcourt defenders and not part of this drill.

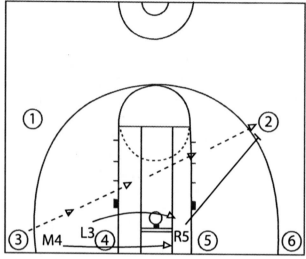

Diagram 12.21